Mindful Money Management

Mindful Money Management

Memoirs of a Hedge Fund Manager

Joel Salomon

ISBN: 0999280406
ISBN 13: 9780999280409

Contents

*Dedicated to all my teachers, and especially my daughters,
Lauren and Morgan, who taught me unconditional love
and continue to teach me every day.*

Introduction

It's 3:30 a.m. on Friday, September 19, 2008. I'm awake and I can't go back to sleep. Again! I'm in a cold sweat. This has been going on for months now. My whole body is dripping wet. I really wish I could remember my dreams. Did something bad happen to my youngest daughter, Morgan (she's only two and a half)? Was it her older sister, Lauren (she's just four and a half)? Was it a stock? A long collapsing? Or a short being acquired? Or something else? What am I fearful of? What am I worried about? Why can't I remember my dreams!?

The last year had been a year of transition for me, both personally and professionally. I had gotten divorced from Christine in December 2007. We had been married in 2002 and we had created two amazing, caring daughters together. But this was my first job in which I got paid based on my performance which was clearly something I had to get used to. I took the job because I was confident in my abilities. But less than nine months later, I was truly questioning them!

This time, at least, I knew why I was wide awake and couldn't go back to sleep. The U.S. Securities and Exchange Commission (SEC) took emergency action the night before to temporarily ban the short-selling of all financial institutions. And I am managing a long/short equity hedge fund[1] that invests only in financial companies! Will I be fired? How can I do my job if I can't hedge?

I contemplated what would happen later that day. None of the scenarios could be described as *good*.

First, I realized we were going to lose a lot of money. It was clearly going to be the worst day of my career.

And then I had an even more horrible thought, if that is even possible. Both my longs and shorts were going to go up—*huge*! I had already hit my total exposure limit on Thursday—the amount that Citi allowed me to manage in total assets.

I decided to walk into my boss' office and ask for more capital—yes, *more*.

Our portfolio was up year-to-date. So I asked, and surprisingly, I was approved.

We spent most of the morning deciding at what prices to buy-back half and what prices to cover the rest of the short positions. Because of the ban, we couldn't short anymore.

---

1 A hedge fund manager is an individual who oversees and makes decisions about the investments in a hedge fund. A hedge fund is an investment fund that pools money from a limited number of wealthy individuals or institutional investors and invests those funds in a variety of assets.

What is Mindful Money Management? It is being present. It is being aware of what is going on in your investments (be they stocks, bonds or real estate) and also being aware of what is going on in the overall marketplace for your investments.

It is making decisions that you have faith in since you have done the work (analysis) and you are confident in the value of the investment over the long-term—say, one-to-three years. This gives you a distinct advantage over those who have to care about weekly or monthly, and sometimes daily, performance (i.e., most professional investors).

Being mindful in money management is not staring at the stock screen all day to take advantage of a small move in a stock, but doing your analysis up front and knowing what the company should be worth under various scenarios so that if the market does go down (or up) a lot you have a prescribed method on how to react.

In this particular case, we did not make rash decisions without considering the fact that nothing had changed in the value of the stocks we were expecting to go down.

Can this help you on your route to financial freedom? Absolutely!

Can mindfulness help you to realize your dreams and desires? Yes!

This book is about the lessons I learned as a hedge fund manager and about being of service to others, not solely about a career as a hedge funder. Included are views into how I, as a hedge fund manager, looked at the world around me during my almost three years of

Joel Salomon

managing money for outside investors. I also share my mindful practices that I used to deal with the various adversities that arose along the way. It is about the various techniques I used to stay happy or become happy during challenging stock market moves and individual company declines.

It is also about how gratitude can work for you and how you can "Act As If" to achieve what you want in life.

Most importantly, as Napoleon Hill said in *The Master Key to Riches,* "Aside from the consideration of what I shall receive for my endeavor to serve you, there is the question of an obligation which I owe the world in return for the blessings that have been bestowed upon me. I did not acquire my riches without the aid of others ... To GET one must first GIVE."

That is the main reason I wrote this book. I want to share with others the growth that occurred as I became a more self-aware and spiritual person while also gaining knowledge about managing investments.

For me, being spiritual is not being religious (going to a synagogue, temple, church or mosque). Spirituality means getting in touch with one's spirit or soul. One can do this many, many different ways. But for me, becoming more spiritual meant doing daily affirmations, meditating, visualizing, and listening to uplifting songs.

One of the most important things I now know is that I had attained definiteness of purpose.

I knew in the 1990s that I wanted to be a hedge fund manager. I thought I could use the fund as a stepping-stone to help individuals by ultimately starting a 40-Act Fund, whereby the same strategy could help individuals through a mutual fund format.

When Charles M. Schwab (as quoted in *The Master Key to Riches*) wanted his first promotion from Mr. Andrew Carnegie, the richest man in the world at the time, Carnegie broadly grinned and replied, "If you have your heart fixed on what you want there is nothing I can do to stop you from getting it."

I realized that if I help others to find their path to happiness and success, it would be profoundly rewarding. I found the best way to adopt the philosophy of individual achievement principles is by teaching it to others. "When a man begins to teach anything, he begins also to learn more about that which he is teaching (Napoleon Hill in *The Master Key to Riches*)."

Chapter 1

● ● ●

Being of Service to Others

"Thomas A. Edison dreamed of a lamp that could be lighted by electricity, went to work on his dream, and despite the fact that he met with ten thousand failures he gave the world that lamp. So, let no one discourage you from dreaming, but make sure you back your dreams with action based on Definiteness of Purpose."

—*Napoleon Hill*

"Shut it down? Shut it down? What? We've worked over three years on building it up and you want to shut it down?"

This was one of my colleagues talking to me in the first week of January 2016.

"I was going to ask you for a raise," they told me!

But, yes, I had made a big decision.

Why? Well, I kept on asking myself a few simple questions after experiencing an *aha moment* at a course I took a few weeks earlier, and again when I came home from that course on a Sunday night:

"Is investing my true purpose on earth?"

"Am I supposed to be helping ultra-high net worth individuals and companies be super-wealthy or am I supposed to be of service to those in need—those who can really gain by my knowledge and experience. And those who can gain not only from my financial acumen, but also from my knowledge of "acting as if"—where, through your own thoughts, you can indeed achieve what you ask for."

And then I asked myself: "Are you being of service to others?"

What does *that* mean?

Well, for the last ten years, I've been asking myself that question.

What am I doing for others?

If I am being selfish and just making money for myself to get material things, how is that being of service to others?

Some years I rationalized it by saying, "Well, I am funding a lot of Lauren's and Morgan's college education," or "I've put money aside for them to use in their twenties," or "I did give to my alma mater this year," or "I did give to the New York Food Bank."

But those amounts were not significant compared to my income. And I didn't feel like I was really helping others directly.

But, as my best friend, Rob Davidsen, reminded me, I was helping others all the time. In 2012 and the first half of 2013 specifically, I would go out of my way to talk to friends, former colleagues, and even acquaintances about my top stock ideas, my rationale for investing in them and what my price targets were. Come to think of it, sometimes I went to dinner with friends and all we did was talk stocks. In fact, they remind me that some of those ideas in 2012 and early 2013 made them a lot of money in 2013 and 2014.

So, though it may have not been significant in terms of monetary contribution, a donation of ideas can be very significant.

As Napoleon Hill said: *"If I give you one of my dollars in return for one of yours, each of us will have no more than he started with; but if I give you a thought in return for one of your thoughts, each of us will have gained a 100% dividend on his investment of time."*

The most important aspect of doing something good, I believe, is how you feel when you do it.

Do you feel happy, or do you feel it is a requirement?

It is similar to when you see people begging for money in the subway. If you feel required to give them money because "it is the right thing to do," should you really give?

If you are doing it because it makes you happy, makes you feel great, makes you feel how grateful you are to have the money you do have, then do it.

I believe this happens in general throughout life. We are focused on what we are observing in our life, not what is going to come into it. Instead of acting 'as if' what you want to happen has already been received (as Rhonda Byrne says in *The Secret*—"Ask, Believe and Receive"), we ask and ask and ask.

And then have doubt that we won't receive it.

We depend on the physical world and observe what is going on around us rather than focusing on the fact that when we ask for something, it is already on its way to us.

So, I realized I could be even more of service to others.

I really wanted to take my knowledge and teach others the steps to financial freedom.

This was in the back of my mind most days every year since 2007.

I thought starting a hedge fund could be a great way to help individuals if I could only get a long enough track record to start a mutual fund afterwards.

But did that happen?

No!

Why?

Was it because I became "bored" or unexcited about investing?

Was it because I stopped loving getting up in the morning and investing other peoples' money?

No!

This is why:

In short, I went to a course in December of 2015 which made me realize that my true purpose in life is helping others become financially free.

And not just high-net-worth individuals that are well on their way to financial freedom, but the upper middle class, the middle class, and the lower middle class. These were people who had limiting beliefs that they could get there. These were people who were fearful about investing in the stock market after losing lots of money in 2008 or 2000. Or they had lost a lot of money in real estate in 2008 and 2009 and didn't want to invest money there!

I realized I could be a great educator of investments, budgeting, and cash flow, while teaching others how to save better, as well as teaching them how to manifest their dreams and desires.

But, why did I start a hedge fund?

And should I have??

Should I have gone through all the years of switching from one 'career' to another?

Should I have decided to take a job that required me to deal with the worst financial crisis since the Great Depression?

And then watch as some of my investments jumped or dropped 10% daily?

Being of service to others is what I wanted to do in whatever form that took. And you'll hear a lot about that in the coming chapters.

Chapter 2

● ● ●

My Dream Job—Or Is It?

I'm going to be discussing my dream jobs in this chapter. There have been a number of them from the time I was a child to my most recent dream in 2015. All of them were somewhat related if you are open-minded.

Let me ask you, what's your dream job? If you could do anything—you just won the lottery—*twice!*—and money is no object, what would you want to do?

Try to answer that question honestly, without self-reproach or thinking what you "should" do. After attending countless networking events and cocktail parties between 2012 and 2016, I have found that is a difficult question for many people to answer. That's okay. I myself, however, answered that question quickly and earnestly.

Today, my dream job involves helping others. That means being of service, educating them on personal finances and investing, and also helping them earn money (directly or indirectly) in the stock market or other investments.

If someone asked me that question twenty years ago, though, my answer would have been "Hedge fund manager." But, I was working as an actuary, having just completed the actuarial exams. I had earned the title of Fellow of the Society of Actuaries (FSA). And I encountered many doubters (about becoming a hedge fund manager)!

At the ripe old age of twenty-eight, I was pigeonholed, as many actuaries were at the time. What I mean by "pigeonholed" is that, at most insurers and actuarial firms, an actuary who wanted to be an investor or a hedge fund manager—or even an equity analyst— would have had a difficult time making that "career change" back in the early 1990s.

I believe that change is much easier today as many actuaries work on Wall Street in various capacities, from rating agency analysts to equity or credit analysts.

However, back in 1992, the idea of me being an investor or a hedge fund manager was not supported by many actuaries inside or outside the company. Yet having worked in a number of departments for New York Life Insurance Company (NYL), including the Asset-Liability Management (ALM) area, as well as taking some courses in the Society of Actuaries curriculum, I found my true passion.

I'm sure this happens to everyone in life. They care too much about what other people say and think, instead of following their inner promptings. My gut or intuition was telling me to focus on what I enjoyed doing—what I was actually doing when I didn't *have* to work. But all the 'experts' were telling me it couldn't be done. At a conference I was at in 2015, the speaker recommended that everyone "Doubt the doubt."

Working in the ALM area of NYL, I used *Bloomberg* to look up bond information, but I realized that I could analyze a stock as well!

And the real fun came when I talked to my manager about stocks. She was enamored with Berkshire Hathaway Inc. (Class A). We debated the merits of the investment. With no Baby Berk Class B shares (about one-thirtieth of the price of Class A shares) at the time, she advised me to scratch together $11,000 and buy a share.

When I started working at New York Life Insurance Company, I had begun a program to "pay myself first"—taking money out of my paycheck every time I was paid and putting it into a separate account. I later realized that was what T. Harv Eker called a "Financial Freedom Account." I began doing this in 1990 just four years after I moved out of my parents' house on Long Island.

I started small, which is what I would recommend everyone do. I began with just $20 a week but eventually by the time I left New York Life, and had become enamored with stock investing and my dream of being a fund manager, I was putting $100 a week into this account.

This helped me invest and compound money—and have my money work for me—for many years.

Today, I recommend that my clients have three to six months of expenses covered before they start investing.

Here is one unique aspect of my coaching: I don't tell people to just invest in the stock market, which is what my passion is. I tell them to consider what limiting beliefs they have. If they are fearful—very scared—of losing money, we first overcome this limiting belief before they invest. And most importantly, I tell them to invest where their passion lies.

This is not something you will find in any finance textbook. Diversification is taught everywhere, all the time. But my opinion is, if you start from a position of concern or fear, then that should be overcome first, before you start with that investment. And if you are fearful of losing money, you will lose money. If, like one client of mine said, "Well if I invest in the stock market, I am just going to lose money," then guess what will happen. Thoughts are indeed "things," and you attract what you fear. And you will lose money!

The law of attraction will not create a positive outcome if you are spending time worrying (I call this negative future planning) about losing money.

So the key question for me in 1993 was how to better align my hobby and career.

My hobby, unbeknownst to my colleagues or supervisors, was analyzing companies.

I had read many books on investing, but the one that truly resonated with me was Marty Zweig's *Winning on Wall Street.* His common-sense approach to looking at economic factors to decide where we are in the economic cycle, and his easy approach to considering the impact of earnings, margins and revenue growth, spoke to a math geek who enjoyed putting together hundreds of rows and columns of numbers.

The book moved me to speak to a number of actuaries who worked at rating agencies and Wall Street firms. The response was nearly unanimous. If you want to move to the buy side—that is, invest in stocks or bonds of insurers—the best place to learn is a rating agency.

Both Moody's Investors Service and Standard and Poor's Rating Service were touted as great training grounds. The Wall Street guys stated it quite simply: "There you would be able to utilize your actuarial skills to analyze financial statements, get access to many insurers' cash flow testing and reserve adequacy analysis, and be able to determine the creditworthiness of those insurers."

Not only that, they said, but you would have the opportunity to upgrade or downgrade companies, assign ratings to debt securities, write up special reports on important industry issues, and create research reports on individual companies.

Additionally, you would be able to travel.

The analysis aspects sounded awesome. The job description also appealed to my second-biggest passion after investing, which is traveling. I was hooked.

So, what to do next?

Abby, my best friend at the time, suggested I send a Federal Express package to the head of the insurance division at Moody's and state "If you give me two minutes of your time, I will show you I am the best candidate for the senior analyst job." That got me an interview.

I went in thoroughly prepared for any actuarial question. I also came prepared to talk about a few ratings that I deemed too high or too low and my favorite assets, stocks and bonds. Hours of preparation made me a confident candidate.

But the head of the insurance group asked me a very telling question. "What is your view of the real estate market and which geographies and types do you think will perform well and poorly in the next few years?"

What?

What does this have to do with all the products insurers sell and how they could be mis-sold?

This young actuary (myself) focused on bonds, stocks and insurance liabilities (reserves for future claim payments) and was not focused on an asset class that in 1991 effectively caused a very large life insurer to be taken over by its regulators.

The division head clearly determined that I was not yet ready for a senior analyst role. But I did manage to secure a junior analyst position. Getting in the door was, of course, the goal. So, I took the job!

One of my earliest memories working at Moody's was when my new boss came into my office, and saw a big smile on my face and a stack of blue books piled high on my desk. "Blue books" was the nomenclature used by analysts and investors for the statutory statements that life and annuity insurance companies filed with individual state regulators. The covers were blue, as opposed to the color of the property and casualty insurers who filed yellow books.

Glancing at the mound of books and work piled in front of me, he asked why I was so happy. I explained to him that "I am getting paid to *analyze* an insurance company. What could be better than that?"

The Plaque Outside Moody's Investors Service in 1995.

My experience at NYL proved invaluable in my initial days at Moody's. The experience working on statutory statements as an actuary helped me flip to where to look for the important disclosures, and the key reserve interest rate assumptions by product type. Not to mention of course, being able to spot the most important scenarios in the insurer's cash flow testing (asset adequacy) reports.

My initial job was to write up research reports on various asset classes and asset-liability management, and to help the senior analysts. Eventually, I was promoted and became responsible for my own portfolio of companies, analyzing each page of those statutory statements, and writing up research on those insurers.

Plus, I got to travel the country.

I visited Pacific Life in Newport Beach, California. While there, I took a detour to La Jolla to put my toes in the sand and savor some of my favorite seafood.

I visited Kansas City, where I conducted a due diligence on a mutual life insurer and had a stellar steak dinner. There were many short overnight trips to St. Louis, Philadelphia, Hartford, Atlanta, and Cincinnati, as well.

Ultimately, these trips to insurers peppered across the country helped me compete with a good friend of mine who was doing a countrywide baseball stadium tour. As of September 2017, I am just one state short of reaching all fifty (Alaska). As they say in the Broadway hit show *Hamilton*, "Just you wait... ".

You might ask me what my top five cities in the United States are. I have included these in Appendix 1.

After nearly four years of excellent experience and acquiring invaluable knowledge across various products and company cultures, I realized my learning curve was leveling off at Moody's. I was one step closer to my dream job of becoming a hedge fund manager.

At the same time, I received a call from an actuarial recruiter who told me that a reinsurer, called Swiss Reinsurance Company (Swiss Re) with headquarters in New York and Zurich, was making private equity (PE) investments and was looking for an analyst. I jumped at the chance to interview and quickly realized during the interview that the job was much more than a PE analyst.

This group at Swiss Re was on the cutting edge of financial markets. They were structuring credit enhancements (a method whereby a company attempts to improve its creditworthiness) for individual insurance blocks of business and trying to do the same for whole companies. And they were managing the existing private equity portfolio.

Now, I realized this wasn't public securities (the kind traded on exchanges, with constantly updated prices like you see crawling across the bottom of the TV screen on CNBC). But I also realized that it was getting me one step closer to my dream job. So, I took it!

My experience at Moody's provided me with an excellent perspective for this department at Swiss Re. I was able to jump right in.

I understood the importance of rating agencies and how to help structure the transaction to achieve the highest ratings. It was also helpful to have worked on analyzing insurers from a credit perspective since the private equity analysis was a long-term investment from another point of view.

Fast-forward to July 1998. I am in the Canadian Rockies with my good friend, Mike Perlin.

We are planning an amazing day of hiking in Banff. I am about to make a critical mistake. I grab a *Financial Times* to read over breakfast. I turn to the second section to see this headline: "Life Re Agrees to Be Bought by Swiss Re." I read the short article and feel my stomach start to ache.

I call my boss at Swiss Re and have to leave a voicemail: "Ed, I saw the news. It doesn't sound good. I know we are purchasing Life Re, but you're not mentioned in the article. Nor is Kin [Ed's boss]. Can you call me back today?" I hang up, not feeling any better.

Some may look back and view it as a "take-under" given the forthcoming changes in management and strategy. It was clear from the announcement to this PE analyst that his division was not "core," as Moody's used to say.

Ed called me back a few hours later and told me: "Joel, I don't disagree with you. Don't be surprised to see a pink slip on your desk when you get back!"

I hang up.

Are you kidding me??

I was at Swiss Re about one year.

I have to look for another job?

Well, those last 10 days of that trip to the Pacific Northwest wasn't my best vacation.

I get back to New York. Happily, there wasn't a pink slip on my desk. But in September 1998, I learned that my whole group was being let go. I did have to look for another job!

Two months later, as I am interviewing for other positions, I get a call from an actuary in another division of Swiss Re. He says, "Joel. I heard what is going on. I think I have a solution. There is a need for an insurance credit analyst in Credit Risk Management. I can put you in touch with the head of the division and I'm sure you will get the job. There is only one catch. The job is in Zurich."

I hung up. Now, you have already heard that one of my biggest passions in life is traveling, and being smack in the center of Europe is probably the best place to start your travels.

So, from bad things come good things, and from really bad things come great things!

And what happened next? The actuary in Swiss Re New Markets who had called me, then hounded the Credit Risk Management Department to woo me.

Getting laid off so that I could move to Zurich wasn't the reason why I joined Swiss Re. But I realized that it was an excellent position to learn about credit risk. Swiss Re was the company actually doing the transactions.

Not only was I excited by the prospect of delving into all types of financial instruments and insurers, but I got to analyze them from Zurich.

Traveling is indeed a passion of mine. But when I first heard that the job had to be in Zurich, I was filled with a mix of joy and fear.

The joy came from the opportunity to travel from the center of Europe. In 1995, I had visited my good friend, Ken Kim, in London with Rob Davidsen. We journeyed from London to Paris on the Chunnel and saw the Eiffel Tower, the Cathedral of Notre Dame, the Louvre, the Rodin Museum and the Picasso Museum. We also ventured out of Paris to see Versailles.

I realized Ken was living my dream life and traveling the world, and I wished for that. Four years later I got my wish.

Everyone has their own Aladdin's lamp and Genie!!

My Genie, I realized, was me! I wished for travel and I got it!

So, why was I nervous and fearful?

Well, I had not lived abroad before. I had no idea about the culture, the people, the language, let alone the work environment. I also didn't know anyone there. I had no support network like I did in New York. Still, I knew that despite the fears, it felt right ("Feel the Fear and Do It Anyway").

Though I was not yet schooled in the learnings of Abraham Hicks or Wayne Dyer, I realized even back then, that it is important to trust your emotions.

I was invited to go to Zurich for three weeks in January 1999 to get acclimated. My new boss certainly knew how to sell me!

She invited me to the annual Swiss Re New Markets conference in Schruns, Austria for an intense few days of note-taking. I arrived a day early to experience skiing Austrian-style. The Swiss know how to balance work and life. I was sold after my first weekend.

I was supposed to be in Zurich for just six months. But how would I be able to get to visit all of my favorite cities in just six months? I needed more time!

In fact, I arrived on April 30th 1999 and by September, I had *only* visited Berlin, the Black Forest, Lisbon, Munich, Venice, Como, Milan, Lugano, Locarno, Bellinzona, Davos, Geneva, Luzern, Basel, Stuttgart, Dachau, Vaduz, London, Bruges, and Brussels.

I was just getting started. I begged to stay longer and my boss complied. I stayed another six months.

Nonetheless, by January 2000, I realized that I still was not going to reach my goal. So, I pleaded once more for an extended stay and I was able to stay until July 2000. I felt somewhat sated, having visited more than twenty European countries, despite not getting my Visa approved in time to visit St. Petersburg, Russia.

I returned to the States, though not without planning a trip back in August to visit Madrid, Barcelona and the Gold Coast of Spain. Happily, I was able to visit all those countries and over forty European cities.

See Appendix 2 for my top five cities in Europe.

It felt boring returning to New York City. I was a newly minted director of a division called Swiss Re Financial Services. As the head of Credit Risk Management in New York, I was still learning a lot about the ever-changing world of credit products. But I also realized that I was not one step closer to my dream job.

In October 2004, I started at Financial Stocks, Inc. (now known as FSI). If someone wanted to analyze insurers, FSI was the place to do it. They were structuring one of the first collateralized debt obligations (CDOs) that included banks and insurers in one pool.

They were also evaluating every private insurer that was raising money in 2004 and 2005 (mainly because of all the storms in 2004 and 2005 including hurricanes Katrina, Rita, and Wilma). And finally, though the hedge fund had invested in insurers in the past, the opportunity to grow this portion of the investments into a majority of the portfolio was just what I wanted.

From there, it was just a matter of time before Citigroup called with my 'almost' dream job. I say 'almost' because I would be working for a large bank and not at a hedge fund or my own hedge fund.

They asked me if I wanted to manage a portfolio on the proprietary desk of the equities division. I would have responsibility for deciding which insurers to buy, sell or short (bet that the stock was going down).

And I would be responsible for sizing the positions and deciding whether the portfolio overall was long or short.

Was I up to the task?

It was the end of 2007. Can anyone say "financial crisis?"

Years of analyzing credit risk helped this actuary know that ultimately, an insurer and other financial institutions are dependent on access to the credit and equity markets for their viability. That helped me, a new portfolio manager, to make money in 2008, when it was not clear to many if *any* financial institutions were creditworthy.

I spent late 2007 and early 2008 reading two books that have changed my life. One was given to me in 2007 by my mother-in-law at the time and is called *The Secret*. The other is *Think and Grow Rich*. Both have interesting stories attached to them.

I was divorced in December 2007 after five years of marriage to Christine. I tell people she has been one of my greatest teachers in my life (because of the improvements I have made in my own life because of her) and, of course, she gave birth to two amazing and beautiful girls, Lauren and Morgan. Lauren was born on February 18th in 2004 and Morgan came almost exactly two years later in 2006 on February 15th.

I started working at Citi the day after Martin Luther King Jr. Day in January 2008. I was all set (or so I thought). I had my few top longs and shorts all set to go.

Unfortunately, I didn't have a Bloomberg machine and the printer wasn't connected. We also had to go through a series of compliance tests before we could start investing. And I had to hire an analyst to work with me. We were responsible for investing in insurers, asset managers, and business development companies.

I started slowly buying just a few companies and shorting just a few as well, but the volatility of those securities was anything but small in the first few weeks. One of my shorts jumped more than 20% before February and we lost hundreds of thousands of dollars! So much for all that research, though ultimately I was proven right on this idea as it dropped more than 50%. It took another eight months for success.

It is important to remember that despite the ultimate 39% drop in the overall market index in 2008 that there were many "bear market rallies." A bear market is one in which the stock market declines 20% or more from its peak. A rally within the bear market could be a jump of 5, 10 or even 25%, though the ultimate trend is still much lower. But we were positioned for the market to go down most days.

I started reading *The Secret* in 2007 but began focusing on work and preparing for my job at Citi in December and January 2008. I picked up *The Secret* again in February and came to a part that really intrigued me. In the book, it talked about this man who thought about this feather. Not any old feather, but a very unique feather with etchings and carvings in it and various colors on it. He thought about it day and night until one day he happened to be walking down the street and saw the feather he had imagined in his mind weeks before.

In the book it then said, "You try!" So, I did. I read that passage in February 2008 and the first thing that popped into my mind after reading it was cotton balls. Pure white cotton balls. I don't know why but that is what popped into my head.

So, starting in February 2008 I began thinking of cotton balls when I woke up and again right before I went to sleep. Every day— day and night.

At the time, Lauren and Morgan were just four and two and I had a double jogging stroller that I used to go jogging with them. When it became warm enough in April, I jogged with them around a local high school track and then to Crawford Park in Rye Brook, New York. I ran up the hill and then to the play- ground. This is where I got my well-deserved five to ten-minute break. I let my little girls out of the stroller and pushed them on the swings and down the slide. Then back into the stroller for the jog back home.

Well, we did this every Saturday and Sunday when I had them in April and May. And on May 31st, we were doing our usual jog. I had pushed my girls up the big hill, arriving at the playground. I was letting them out of the stroller when I looked down and saw all over that playground, hundreds of cotton balls.

I was in a state of shock as I screamed at Lauren and Morgan to pick up as many as they could. I had been believing for months that I would see cotton balls and yet when I did finally see them (and of course, not just one or two but tons of them!), I was quite surprised.

But once I finally got over the shock, a feeling of joy and bliss came over me. Wow, this does indeed work. It did take some time—over three months in my case—but they did show up!

For years after, I had a sand-covered cotton ball at my desk at work to remind me that thoughts are indeed "things." You can, without a doubt, manifest physical things into reality.

This is what is called manifesting (For a more detailed discussion of manifesting, check out the Programs dropdown menu on JoelSalomon.com).

An important early lesson at Citi was that almost everything is about expectations.

On the Friday before St. Patrick's Day—March 17th—Bear Stearns Corporation (BSC) was teetering. It had already collapsed from $159 to just under $60 in less than a year, but on Friday, March 14th, it dropped almost 50%—*in one day*—to about $30. I remember a colleague of mine at the time sending an email on March 16th —Sunday—saying how J.P. Morgan had proposed to take BSC over for $2. I immediately responded back saying how I think he had missed a "0," but alas he hadn't. The price was $2, not $20.

And what happened? The market partied like it was 1999. Two days later the market index was up 3.3%. A week after, it was up almost 5%.

Why? One word: Expectations!

Apparently, unbeknownst to this wet-behind-the-ears portfolio manager, a $2 price (which incidentally was revised a week later to $10) was better than what was expected. And that was *zero*.

You see, most investors "in the know" were expecting BSC to be declared bankrupt over the weekend and they were not expecting *any* buyers to step in. Apparently that is how bad the situation was.

Now, unfortunately, my portfolio was positioned for bad news. That means that we had more shorts than longs and were effectively expecting the market to go down more than up over the coming weeks and months.

That did not happen. I called this first bear market rally from March 17th to May 19th the "Bear Stearns rally." It lasted more than two months, during which time the market jumped almost 11%!

During this time, I also met a woman who changed my life!

We met through one of the online websites. I think it was Match.com or eHarmony.com. During the first date, she mentioned that she was a big fan of Napoleon Hill and his New York Times Best Seller, *Think and Grow Rich* (in fact, by 2015, there had been more than one hundred million copies of the book sold worldwide!).

She asked me if I had heard of him. I hadn't. We had a wide-ranging discussion. Not only was she quite beautiful, but she was intelligent and spiritual. And most importantly, she offered to give me a copy of *Think and Grow Rich* when we met again! A second date! This would be my first second date after having been divorced. I was excited, to say the least.

The next time we met, she not only brought *Think and Grow Rich*, but also *The Master Key to Riches* and *The Law of Success in Sixteen Lessons*! All by Napoleon Hill.

Wow—she was thoughtful, giving, intelligent *and* beautiful. I was smitten.

There was only one problem.

After the second date, I never saw her again!

She didn't respond to my calls, texts or emails!

I was *so* upset. What had I done?

It took me many months to get over this rejection, but I realized years later that she was an angel who came into my life to change me and make me a better person.

I was so distraught, that for most of 2008 I couldn't even pick up any of the books she had given me.

But I finally decided to read *Think and Grow Rich* in December. And twice a year since!

The positive energy it exudes, the uplifting stories, and the life lessons are invaluable. If you haven't read it, go online to joelsalomon.com, and I will send you one of the copies I keep around my house!

Back to 2008 and the crazy volatility that I experienced.

In May 2008, American International Group (AIG) announced they were raising capital. Most investors in financials knew this was coming. However, the big open question during late April and early May was, "How much?"

Our estimate was the amount would likely be between $5 billion and $10 billion. AIG in fact, raised more than $13 billion. My initial reaction was, "This must be good news!"

If they were able to raise so much more than our initial estimate then that should be a good thing, right?

But again what were expectations?

And how much did they really need?

AIG's stock dropped another 10% from the day after they raised capital—when the dilution (existing holders of the stock have their share 'diluted' because they own less of the company when the company issues more shares) caused a drop in the stock of almost 5%.

Why? Well, many investors expected AIG to have an even bigger need for capital in the future (which was eventually borne out in September 2008), and they felt this was not nearly enough to plug a very big hole in AIG's balance sheet.

This sentiment did not help the overall market's emotional state nor did the numerous downgrades by rating agencies that were going on in the late spring and early summer of 2008.

There was also speculation that two large housing authority stocks that the government effectively guaranteed, Fannie Mae (FNM) and Freddie Mac (FRE), were near insolvency. This expectation and sentiment proved false—at least temporarily.

In June 2008, after I had "manifested" the cotton balls in Crawford Park that May, I went back to the book, *The Secret,* and printed out the check they recommended you should print out from their website, thesecret.tv.

It read "The Gratitude Bank of the Universe; Drawer: The Gratitude Bank of the Universe; Account: Unlimited Balance; and Signed: The Universe." It recommended you put an amount on that check that is large, but an amount you don't have significant doubt about. And then, of course, they recommend "Acting As If" by feeling grateful for the money as though you already have it and imagining yourself spending it on something you want in particular.

Well, I put that check up on my ceiling in June 2008 and got up every morning and said "I don't know how; I don't know why—but I *do* know it is coming." See, once I had manifested the cotton balls, I knew the same energy that had created them also creates money. So, every night before I went to sleep, I said to myself, "I don't know how; I don't know why—but I *do* know it is coming."

Chapter 3

● ● ●

Mindfulness

What is mindfulness and how can it be applied to money? This chapter gives some examples of how you can be mindful when managing money—how to be present when you want to crawl into a hole! How to overcome adversity when it feels like nothing is going your way.

From the day AIG raised capital in May until the low in July, the overall stock market had an almost 12% downdraft.

But when the rumors of FNM and FRE's demise were deemed unfounded in late July, the bear market had another of its hurtful (for those who were expecting the market to indeed collapse) rallies.

From the low in July, the overall market rallied more than 5%. But then the collapse of Lehman Brothers (LEH) occurred in early September with all the inherent counterparty credit risks associated with it, including some insurers that were not well capitalized, like AIG.

I remember being out for dinner on City Island in the Bronx on September 14th with my mother and father for my mom's birthday, when my blackberry started lighting up at dinner.

Was this even possible?

The government was going to allow Lehman Brothers to go down?

Hadn't they thought about the consequences?

Apparently not!

The almost 5% drop in the stock market was not more, only because there was a lot of speculation that the government was stepping in and going to do something big.

The Federal Reserve was cutting interest rates which also helped stem the decline, but I was confused.

My strongly held belief was (and is) that governments should not manipulate markets.

Wouldn't it be worse if the government did something to stop the market decline?

Wouldn't it just defer the inevitable?

Apparently that was not the thought, because on the evening of September 18th something unprecedented in the U.S. stock market happened.

I was having a dinner with an asset manager analyst and another five or six fellow portfolio managers and analysts, when someone announced in the middle of dessert that the U.S. government had banned short selling in all financial institutions.

What?

How could they do that?

And really?

Is that a solution to a financial crisis?

Treat a symptom of the problem, not the problem itself. To me, the problem was banks and other financial institutions didn't have enough money to cover their losses from mortgages and other credit related loans. Providing low-cost funding to these financial institutions—which the government ultimately did in 2009—was the solution. *Not* regulating the stock market.

I remember not sleeping that night, thinking I'm out of a job.

How can I be a hedge fund manager without any hedges??

I thought about this long and hard overnight. The other thought I kept on having was how much money we were going to lose that day. We had more shorts than longs on that day of September 19th—by a lot! It was clearly going to be the worst day of my career.

And then I had an even more horrible thought. Both my longs and shorts were going to go up—*huge*! I had already hit my total exposure limit on Thursday—the amount that Citi allowed me to manage in total assets.

I decided to walk into my boss' office and ask for more capital— yes, *more.*

Our portfolio was up year-to-date. So, in some ways, I was in a position of power (I think there was only one other portfolio manager that was up through mid-September) and of course, they didn't know how bad September 19th was going to be for our portfolio (only *I* did!).

So I asked, and surprisingly, we were approved. I made only one trade that day. We sold one of our long positions that was heavily shorted. It had jumped more than 50% by 9:45 a.m. and we were able to sell 1,000 shares before it started collapsing. It was a pittance compared to our more than 25,000 shares, but it felt good. However, we did indeed have a horrible day.

After 10:00 a.m., my analyst and I decided to take a walk outside. We really couldn't take any action anyway and it was a beautiful late summer day. So we walked around the block and decided on a plan of action. We realized nothing fundamentally had changed and more likely than not, it was going to get worse before it got better. We liked our conservative longs and didn't want to sell them, but we did expect our shorts to collapse.

So, we spent most of the morning deciding at what prices to cover half and what prices to cover the rest of the short positions. Since we were already "max" short, we couldn't sell any longs, and of course—because of the ban—we couldn't short anymore anyway.

• • •

What is Mindful Money Management? It is being present. It is being aware of what is going on in your investments (be they stocks, bonds or real estate) and also being aware of what is going on in the overall market.

Have the fundamentals of the stock changed? This means has there been some new piece of information about the company you are invested in that would change its value? Or is there soon to be news—are they about to report their earnings or announce a new product launch or release a new drug? If not, and there is a big move in the stock, is it based on the overall market movement?

Now, some stocks are "equity-market sensitive" which means that they own stocks in their investment portfolio directly impacting their stock value, or they are insurance companies having sold products tied to the stock market. Let's put those companies aside for now.

If the stock (or the underlying company) is not one of those, and it goes down more than the overall stock market, it is likely technical or emotional. That is, there are a lot more sellers than buyers at that price, and the stock price has to drop to find more buyers.

If it is just emotional—fear—then being present, and knowing that the company's value has not changed, is being mindful. You can be a willing buyer knowing that the stock might not rebound in a day or two or even a month, and that's fine as long as you're focused on the long-term value of the firm and you are indeed an investor, like I am.

Making decisions you have faith in because you've already done the work (analysis) and now have confidence in the value of the company over the long-term (say, one-to-three years), gives you a distinct advantage over those who have to care about weekly or monthly performance (i.e., most professional investors).

Being mindful in money management is not staring at the stock screen all day to take advantage of a small move in a stock. It is doing your analysis up front and knowing what the company should be worth under various scenarios so that if the market does go down (or up) a lot, you have a prescribed method on how to react.

In this particular case, we did not make rash decisions without considering the fact that nothing had changed in the overall value of the stocks we were expecting to go down.

Mindfulness is defined as "The quality or state of being conscious or aware of something." It is also defined as "A mental state achieved by focusing one's awareness on the present moment, while calmly acknowledging and accepting one's feelings, thoughts, and bodily sensations, used as a therapeutic technique."

In Buddhism, mindfulness is utilized to develop self-knowledge and wisdom which gradually leads to what is described as enlightenment or the complete freedom from suffering. The popularity of mindfulness in the West is generally considered to have been initiated by Jon Kabat-Zinn.

Mindfulness, to me, is also about recognizing your feelings, thoughts, and body sensations.

If you are feeling sad, depressed, or upset, you are probably not in the best state to get the items you want in your life.

On the other hand, if you are happy, ecstatic, having fun or laughing, you are more likely to get what you want. Knowing your feelings and your thoughts can help you make better decisions. And that is being mindful!

A great example of mindfulness comes from the well-known book, *Man's Search for Meaning*, by Viktor Frankl. Viktor was a concentration camp survivor and explained how he was able to rise "above the situation" by doing the following: "I became disgusted with the state of affairs ... [which] forced my thoughts to turn to another subject. Suddenly, I saw myself standing on the platform of a well-lit, warm and pleasant lecture room ... I was giving a lecture on the psychology of the concentration camp! All that oppressed me at the moment became objective, seen and described from the remote viewpoint of science. By this method I succeeded somehow in rising above the situation, above the suffering for the moment, and I observed them as if they were already in the past."

Viktor was able to develop freedom from suffering, albeit for just a few minutes, by taking his mind out of the current situation and seeing it from the future. As he stated "emotion, which is suffering, ceases to be suffering as soon as we form a clear and precise picture of it."

• • •

Unfortunately for the U.S. and the market, we were right and the ban only delayed the inevitable. Between the date of the ban and its lifting, the stock market collapsed almost 28%.

Another very memorable experience from September 2008 was from our largest position. We had invested in a stock we considered "safe." It actually benefited from heightened foreclosures and its investment risk was much, much lower than most of the industry.

Furthermore, it had held up extremely well. It was only down 3% through early September. Then "something" happened!

On "Lehman day", it declined like all insurers and financial stocks about 5%. But the following days were even more brutal and despite the jump when short selling was banned, it dropped almost 10% in the following days. We didn't employ stop losses (see JoelSalomon.com for a discussion of Stop Losses under Programs in the Investing Section) and, thus, we continued to hold on to our highest-conviction idea. This was clearly wrong!

In October, the position collapsed another 54%. No, that is not a typo! It dropped more than half. And we held on…and on…and on.

Until we made the decision to reduce the whole portfolio, we did not sell any of this position.

Another great lesson learned from my time at Citi was to trust my gut or use my intuition. I hadn't really explored doing this for most of my life (at least consciously), but I found in 2008, that many times when I had a feeling something was about to happen—with a stock, or in the overall market—it did.

I tried to work on figuring out what stock would jump or decline, but I found it easier to try to feel the overall market movement. See, the market is just a voting machine. If most investors/speculators are fearful, the market is likely to go down. If they are greedy or ecstatic, it is likely to go up.

Most days in 2008—excluding those bear market rallies—the fear was palpable. Not only from my colleagues all around me, but just by watching the tickers on my screen, I really felt that fear.

2008 was the year I learned how to use this skill just like you would use any other skill—like credit analysis, equity analysis or risk management. As I used it more and more, I became increasingly confident that the decisions I made based on my intuition were good ones.

Some people say intuition is just using all the knowledge you've accumulated in your lifetime. I found my intuition helped me make money, and when I didn't trust it, I tended to make less money or lose it.

The final bear market rally started not long after the ban was lifted, perhaps contrary to what many expected. It took just a few weeks before the rally began in earnest—a 21% jump, for those counting—in just a month's span from mid-November to mid-December.

The amount of intestinal fortitude it took to handle these huge swings is really impossible to convey to the reader. Thankfully, we had made a decision to take our amount of invested assets down in early November, seeing as we had made a tiny amount of money for the firm and ourselves. It was also a bit unsettling to see all our colleagues doing research and not investing because their exposure had been reduced or eliminated by management.

Plus, it was difficult to deal with the fact that 25% of the workforce at Citi was laid off in late November, including four of our colleagues in the Equity Principal Strategies division!

My former colleagues tell me that one of my claims to fame should be that we made money in September 2008—we were up 0.1%, but positive is positive—despite the ban on short selling in financial institutions. And of course, the stock market collapsed about 9.5% that month.

Why did this happen?

Well, at least for a couple of weeks, insurance company investors were considering the potential for a very hard market. This means that premiums or the prices that consumers and companies have to pay their insurers will go up dramatically.

Why?

Well if the largest insurance company in the U.S., American International Group, is going to fail or need substantial assistance from the United States Government, the overall market and especially AIG should increase prices. This was the thought for about two or three weeks. And on my stock screen from mid-September until early October, the only stocks that were green (going up) were property and casualty insurers and their brokers. They benefited from higher premiums because brokers' commissions are paid as a percentage of premiums earned or written.

I'd be remiss if I didn't mention the other claim to fame my former colleagues harp on whenever I see them. In 2008, the overall stock market dropped about 38%. That is, the average investor who put $1,000 into the market on December 31st, 2007, ended the year with just $620. If an investor was enamored with financial stocks at the end of 2007, they would have lost even more—approximately 55%! This means if they had put $1,000 into a widely used financial stock index, they would have had just $450 at the end of the year. The portfolio I managed was positive by a few per cent. That is, if you had your money in my portfolio that year, you would have had more than $1,000 at the end of the year.

We started 2009 with a very small amount of assets to invest. And we slowly added longs and shorts in January. Unfortunately, our best short idea collapsed 20% from its peak in early January in three short weeks, and yet we had less than 1% of our total allowable short position in it.

2009 was another year of learning many valuable (though painful!) lessons. We continued to be negative much longer than we should have been.

The bear market "ended" on March 9th when Citi's CEO at the time, Vikram Pandit, declared the company would be profitable in the first quarter of 2009. Lots of other factors were clearly at work as well, but when a major bank that had traded below one dollar a few days before (compared to more than $55, just two years earlier) declares it is profitable, the impact can't be measured.

The bond market was also healing and some companies were able to issue bonds at what they considered "not outrageous prices."

My own portfolio was not positioned at all for the stock market rally that began that day, but eventually the light bulb went on as I saw the clear trend in the bond market in late April.

By that time, I began adding to my favorite business development company. This whole sector of the market is a levered credit investment like real estate. This means that as the credit market improves, they benefit many times more than the actual improvement because their equity is only 10% or less of their assets. So, their assets are more than 10 times their equity.

The decision to add to this position when the equity market dipped starting in April paid huge dividends in August of 2009, when it had become the biggest position of the fund. We had analyzed the underlying investments and saw how positively they would impact equity.

When the company reported that its book value had indeed appreciated by more than 20%, the stock jumped more than 21%. We made 1.8% on the whole portfolio just that day! Some colleagues told me this was quite an unusual feat especially given the fact that we were managing a well-diversified portfolio which was only taking 20% of the market risk. If you annualized that 1.8%, you would have a return of approximately 50,000%!

August 2009 was the most profitable month of my career. Besides this huge gain, the portfolio benefited from a benign catastrophe season (there was little damage from hurricanes) and the reinsurers in the portfolio jumped. We had also been able to invest in fixed income securities (bonds) that leapt dramatically from late spring. We were able to sell them in late August and early September with gains of more than 50%.

In 2009, we had our best year managing money. We were up more than 20% on allocated capital.

But a funny thing happened that year. I actually was spending a lot of time outside the office enjoying my life. I found out how important it was to be happy. Remember my discussion of "Mindful Money Management" earlier. Knowing how you feel and what you are thinking is the first step to manifesting or having a thought become a physical reality.

This was my first time recognizing a limiting belief I had: "You must work hard to be rich and successful." I am pretty sure this is a statement that almost everyone I know—from successful hedge fund managers to actuaries and credit analysts—believe.

But I found it to be a limiting belief and I started thinking about how I could make a lot of money if I was happier. I purposely spent less time analyzing companies and more time doing other fun things like going out on a date, or focusing on Lauren and Morgan more when I was with them.

I remembered that, in 2008, I was not focused on them on the weekends when I had them. I invariably would be reading some analysis or research that I had received over the weekend. In 2009, I became more focused on them and I have been more "present" with them since then.

I also became more mindful at work.

In 2008, I was spending fourteen hours a day focused on my portfolio and most weeks I was working more than seventy hours. In 2009, I purposely reduced this intensity. I was not getting into work at 7:15 a.m. or 7:30 a.m. like I did in 2008 and I did not stay to 8:00 p.m. as I had done most nights that year, either.

I made plans to go out most Tuesdays and Thursdays and not to a business dinner with a company we were invested in, as I had done in 2008.

Nor did I spend as much time going to "ideas dinners." These dinners, during which investors gave their thesis for their best long and short idea, were so common back in 2008 and 2009 that I could spend two or three nights every month going to them. I enjoyed the interaction with other "buy-siders" and the meal was usually an excellent steak or seafood place in midtown Manhattan, but we worked hard on coming up with our own ideas, and the ones that were shared rarely changed our view of the stock or company. We would get concerned, however, when we went to these dinners and two or three other analysts all "pitched" an idea that we were invested in—suddenly making our "unique" and "contrarian" investment anything but.

Did working less and spending time on fun have anything to do with my superior performance?

I believe so!

"Past performance is no guarantee of future results." Some of you may be familiar with this term stamped on the cover of almost every mutual fund advertisement. But this can be applied to many experiences in life.

A recent client talked to me about how hard it was for her to make money after getting divorced. She had earned $50,000 prior to the divorce, and once she was divorced found it hard to make more than that $50,000. She rationalized that "Well, this is what I have 'always' earned so I am unlikely to generate a lot more."

What I told her and what I tell everyone is "past performance is no guarantee of future results." Just because you are making $50,000 a year doesn't mean you will make $50,000 a year the rest of your life. I am a prime example of this. Though my "money thermostat" was clearly set for less than $150,000 for years, I figured it out early enough to "break through."

In the first twenty years of my career, whenever I went above that amount I somehow rationalized a shift in my career was worthy of a pay cut back below that amount. This happened after leaving New York Life Insurance Company and again after leaving Swiss Reinsurance Company.

In fact, when I realized I had subconsciously programmed myself to not go much above this number, I was able to reprogram myself to dramatically higher amounts at Citigroup (as I tell people, "multiples of what I had made earlier in my career for consecutive years").

Again, "past performance is no guarantee of future success."

> *"If you are one of those people who believes that*
> *hard work and honesty alone will bring riches,*
> *perish the thought. It is not true! Riches, when they*
> *come in huge quantities, are never the result of hard*
> *work...**Ideas** are the beginning of all fortunes."*
>
> —NAPOLEON HILL

In January 2010, my boss at Citigroup called me into a conference room. He said "Joel, you had a good year last year." He then slipped an envelope to me which I opened. I was amazed—but not amazed—to see the amount of the check that I had on the ceiling in my bedroom the last eighteen months.

Manifesting works like that.

First, you have a thought; then you *know* it will become a physical reality, and then you have the feeling of it.

Wayne Dyer said: "Make your future dream a present reality by assuming the *feeling* of the wish fulfilled." Before I had even read *Wishes Fulfilled*, I did that!

In 2009, the stock market had rebounded quite nicely, up about 26%. The financial stocks that we had invested in did slightly worse, up 17% based on one common index. Our performance was similar to the overall stock market—better than financial stocks—and some may say a heroic performance because we were taking less than 50% of the market risk. Thus we should have, theoretically, been up less than half the market, assuming our stock picking ability added no additional return.

In 2010, I had another successful year. Though we generated a return just under 5%, our relative market exposure of 20% or so implied that we should have been up around 2.3% (20% of the 11.5% return that the overall stock market index achieved). And managing a lot more money—actually almost double the amount we managed in 2008 and 2009—was a challenge unto itself.

Other challenges abounded. The volatility (meaning big swings in stock prices) in individual securities did not abate. I remember one fateful day in the spring of 2010 when I was attending a lunch meeting with an asset manager, AMG (Affiliated Managers Group). Our normal expert traders were out that day and we had a young trader "subbing."

I left for my lunch in midtown Manhattan around 11:15 a.m. These midtown lunch meetings were usually quite informative, but they also took a big chunk out of my day since we were based all the way downtown on Greenwich Street in now-trendy Tribeca.

It is interesting to note that when Sandy Weill built this downtown headquarters of Citigroup for Shearson Lehman (later purchased by Travelers) in 1989, that Tribeca was anything but trendy. The cost was a tiny fraction of the $1.6 billion sale price that the building sold for in 2007.

So, I am at this AMG lunch about to partake of the salmon entrée when my boss texts me over Bloomberg instant messenger (which I "happened" to be glancing at under the table—"there are no coincidences") asking me, "What are you going to do about Lender Processing Services (LPS)?"

Unbeknownst to me, LPS was now under legal investigation as a press release announcing this information had informed the world, while I was listening to AMG management talk about the benefits of their business model.

Why our trader hadn't noticed the 18% drop in a short hour is still confounding to me.

And how did my boss, who was also head of all of Equities for Citi, happen to notice my 3% position in LPS? I was truly grateful though. He gave me the chance to call around and try to get more information. Again, this is being mindful—not making a rash decision when you have no information, nor simply reacting to a stock price movement.

But what is the "proper" response to an 18% drop when you have limited information?

I could:

(1) sell all of LPS—take the loss and move on (our stop loss criteria was based on end of day values; thus, I was not required to do anything at the moment);

(2) hold it all and wait for more information; or

(3) sell a portion—half, one third, or two thirds arbitrarily to reduce our "exposure" to this event risk stock.

The third option is what some in the industry term "halfsies." It is a way to make a decision so you can't be wrong! If the stock rebounds over the coming days, you still own some. If it declines further, well, at least you sold some!

Options one and two require you to make an uninformed decision with limited information, so the likelihood of being wrong is high. These types of decisions go on all day long on the trading floors of every major bank. I just didn't make them too often, and when I did I abhorred them.

So, I weaseled out.

I sold half.

LPS continued to swoon in the coming weeks. We eventually sold the other half of the position with an even larger loss, without hitting our ultimate, worst-case stop loss.

Three years later in 2013, LPS sold to Fidelity National Financial, Inc. for $33.25, a price more than 50% higher than where we sold it. Of course, I had sold all the shares I had owned in 2010 before February 2012 when I left Citi.

• • •

When a hedge fund gets too big, it's harder to get in and out of the market. It is harder to buy and sell investments quickly and easily, and being slow means lower returns. Thus, I found there were diminishing returns at Citi as we got bigger and bigger.

But my experience at Citi was invaluable and I met many amazing portfolio managers and analysts. They helped me achieve dramatic success.

After "paying myself first" for almost twenty years while investing the money wisely—and then having two years in which I was able to make a large sum of money—I was able to become financially free. Though, of course, I wanted to continue to do what I loved—investing and helping others.

What does financial freedom mean to you? To me, it means being able to do the things I love when I want to do them.

Today, I help clients calculate their "financial freedom number." That is the amount they would need to have in investments (passive income ideas which include real estate, stocks, currencies, commodities, bonds, side businesses, joint ventures, and hedge funds) to cover their annual expenses.

For example, assuming your expenses don't increase annually and you had monthly expenses of $5,000 per month or $60,000 a year, your financial freedom number is $1,000,000. This assumes you can earn an average of 6% per year. You can also calculate your financial freedom number based on your dream expenses, which means how much expenses you would have annually living your dream life with your dream house, car, and other material items, along with your dream job.

Because of all those years of paying myself first and investing wisely—then having two good performance years at Citi—I was able to fully fund both Lauren's and Morgan's college education. This also allowed me to set up a trust for each of them, buy my parents a condominium in Florida and give to my favorite charities.

What would you do if you were financially free?

What are your dream vacations?

Getting back to my time at Citi—why did I leave?

Well, the Dodd-Frank law passed, creating a "Volcker" rule, which required almost every U.S. bulge bracket investment bank to let go of their proprietary desk portfolio managers. These are the largest and most profitable multi-national investment banks in the world, whose banking clients are normally huge institutions, corporations, and governments.

This meant that my whole group at Citi was going to have to be laid off, which actually happened in February 2012.

The Volcker rule happily led me, finally, some may say, to my dream job.

So, I was able to achieve my "almost" dream job at Citi.

How? Why?

Well, I didn't give up and there was definitely a "method to my madness." I *knew* getting credit analysis and private equity experience would be invaluable to becoming a hedge fund manager. I *knew* that working at a hedge fund as an analyst was a necessary precursor to actually managing money.

And the experience (some may say wasted time!) at Swiss Re in Zurich, and back in New York as a Credit Risk Manager, were also invaluable. Despite already having credit analysis experience at Moody's, I was able to work on new-fangled products—as I did at FSI—that served me well when the credit crisis hit in 2008. I knew where the large risks were. And I was able to be a better stock investor because of that.

Of course, 2008 was not the best time to start being a professional money manager. But that really tough, stressful experience allowed me to make money in 2009 and subsequent years. Then, when stocks starting moving 3% or 4% or 5%, I was able to harken back to 2008 and early 2009 and say to myself, "This is nothing. They have no idea what I went through!" This mentality would prove priceless in future years.

Chapter 4

●　●　●

Acting As If!

It was December 17, 2012. I had just moved into my new office—ultra-prime Manhattan real estate—and could still smell the fresh white paint on the walls as I hung my diplomas. My Dell computer, with the requisite four screens (minimum) for a hedge fund manager (me!!), easily booted up. I sat behind my brand-new desk looking out over a total of five desks (I had space for four more employees). I had an amazing view of bustling 54th Street, just off fashionable Madison Avenue. It felt like I had arrived.

There was one minor problem. Actually, minor is an understatement. The investors' money I thought I was going to be investing in two weeks was nowhere to be found.

SaLaurMor (named after my daughters) was a long/short equity and credit hedge fund focused on financial institutions with a specific bent on—you guessed it—insurance companies.

Service providers are a key element to any hedge fund in this post-Bernie Madoff world. Each fund has a prime broker, fund administrator, auditor, law firm, and of course, the obligatory compliance firm. So, one of the key challenges to a start-up hedge fund is ensuring the proper controls are in place to run the business with appropriate governance. As a passionate investor, having someone whose sole responsibility is handling the business side eases concerns of both existing and potential investors.

It has been said that today no one can start a hedge fund in a garage with a *Bloomberg* machine. So, clearly, start-up (and ongoing) costs were higher because of the cost of hiring a compliance company and the necessity of having a fund administrator to check the fund's daily net asset value. Registering with the Securities and Exchange Commission (SEC) when the fund has $150 million in regulated assets under management, was something that didn't exist ten years ago.

I had been negotiating with two insurers for most of the fall of 2012. The pair recognized their investment returns were under pressure. Both knew they needed to think about diversification. They knew that a low-risk strategy with minimal stock market risk and low correlation to the overall market, financials, and insurance companies made sense.

Correlation of assets is defined as a measure of how much investments move in relation to one another, and when. When assets move in the same direction at the same time, they are considered to be positively correlated. When one asset tends to move up and the other down, the two assets are considered to be negatively correlated.

This way, when the overall stock market falls sharply, their portfolio declines less—or not at all.

Despite my extensive experience and successful track record, my potential new investors voiced myriad objections.

"How can we be sure the track record you have at Citi will be consistent with what you do at your new fund?"

"What is your infrastructure?"

"Who is responsible for managing the business side while you invest our money?"

"Won't we be more than 90% of the fund, therefore, requiring us to consolidate your hedge fund on our financial statements?"

"Why should we have to pay fees?"

And on and on.

Suffice it to say, my pipeline of insurance company investors, the ones who trusted me and the ones who understand my process, decided not to invest.

So there I was, approaching 2013 with no clear route to actually having my own hedge fund. But I had made the commitment to move into commercial real estate space and I had to start paying my real estate broker in January. Did I make a big mistake?

Earlier in 2012, I had met one of many angels who entered my life in the last five years. Paul Pompeo was an avid fan of self-help author Napoleon Hill. He was giving away Hill's top-selling book, *Think and Grow Rich,* to acquaintances and long-time friends alike. We bumped into each other at a Meetup group entitled, "The Power of the Mastermind," based on Chapter 10 in Hill's book. This book became a sort of bible for me after reading it more than ten times since 2008. However, this meetup was nothing like what was suggested in the book.

As Hill explained it, "The Master Mind may be defined as co-ordination of knowledge and effort, in a spirit of harmony, between two or more people for the attainment of purpose." He cited the example of how the Ford Motor Company was essentially started from a mastermind group consisting of Henry Ford, Mr. Ford's wife, Clara Bryant, Thomas Edison, Harvey Firestone, John Burroughs and Luther Burbank.

This Meetup was no 'Ford mastermind,' as Pompeo and I very quickly realized. Politely, we walked out soon after we split into groups of four to five. But I realized soon after, as did Pompeo, that the real reason we met—this *synchronicity*—was to form our own Meetup group based on "The Power of the Mastermind." The aim was to see if we could build a joint venture of some kind or expand our knowledge base in a spirit of harmony to help each other achieve our goals in life.

So Pompeo and I, and eventually another eight enlightened people, met each week in Manhattan to see how we could help each other achieve our dreams. Though no joint venture was consummated, the suggested book readings alone changed my view of the world.

Some of the books members suggested included:

* *Feel the Fear and Do it Anyway* by Susan Jeffers. This book discusses how your lack of trust in yourself can be stopping you from getting what you want out of life and how to change it. I've been quoting from this book to Lauren and Morgan since I read it in 2012. How many parents tell their kids before they go to school: "Take a risk today, Darling?"

* *Secrets of The Millionaire Mind* by T. Harv Eker. Harv gets into the psychology of money. He discusses your money blueprint and whether you are set for success or failure and introduces seventeen wealth files which describe exactly how rich people think and act differently from poor and middle-class people. This is a must-read for anyone who is already financially free or wants to become that way.

* *The Science of Being Rich* by Wallace Wattles. This classic, written in 1910, may be composed in an old style, but is another must-read. The energy that exudes from the typeface (or the mp3 for those who prefer the audio file) feels similar to me to *Think and Grow Rich.* You just feel better after reading it.

* *How to be Wildly Wealthy Fast* by Sandy Forster. Sandy writes with such ease and flow that you can't wait to read more. This book has specific exercises, lessons, and takeaways that translate into action steps. Her abundance breath and affirmations became requirements of the members of the mastermind group soon after we read it. You won't be disappointed.

* *The Art of Happiness* by Dalai Lama XIV. Though it might be a bit long for many readers, I would recommend plowing through to the end. The Dalai Lama, as interviewed by Dr. Howard Cutler, brings insights that you can apply to your daily life. He provides lessons on how to defeat daily issues of anxiety, insecurity, anger, and disappointment.

* *The Magic of Thinking Big* by David Schartz. Another book containing specific action steps that won't become outdated, even though it was originally written more than fifty years ago. The positive attitude flows from this book just like *The Science of Being Rich*. Mastermind members started using David's powerful daily affirmation soon after reading this one as well. Go to JoelSalomon.com (see the Manifesting program for this free affirmation download) for the powerful daily affirmation that David recommends putting on your bathroom mirror so you can see it every morning.

* *Angels in My Hair* by Lorna Byrne. Lorna takes us through her childhood in Ireland and requires you to think big! She tells about her vivid encounters and conversations with angels and spirits which she's had from childhood until the present. Keep an open mind and open heart, and then her message of hope and love can be life-altering.

* *Radical Forgiveness* by Colin Tipping. Paul Pompeo recommended this book to the group and I am so grateful. Colin gets you to think differently about life and why we are here. His view is that our soul is here to be healed and the arguments, anger, and fights you have had are because your soul needs to be healed on that particular issue that you are arguing about. The resolution, amazingly enough, does not require any participation from the other party. Colin even provides worksheets to do whenever a difficult situation

arises. I can vouch for the benefit of them, having completed many a worksheet over the last five years.

* *Throw out Fifty Things* by Gail Blanke. It is amazing how cleaning out clutter from your house can help your mind to also become clearer. Gail takes you through every room in your house to make your house and mind neater and clearer. I finally took her advice and cleaned out half my garage and half my closet. An easy and fun read that also has some specific action steps along that way.

A key takeaway from meeting Pompeo was that everyone should think about going to seminars to add to their personal education and invest in themselves. Pompeo sold me on T. Harv Eker and his course, MMI—The Millionaire Mind Intensive.

I signed up for the course that was held in New Jersey in December 2012, and tried to keep an open mind. Pompeo warned me that while the course was free, there would be a lot of pressure to buy additional courses. But if I could be open to that, he explained, there would definitely be some great learnings, inspirations, and surprises.

Surprises, indeed! Not only were there team-building exercises, there were also relationship and self-love exercises, in which we focused on improving our self-esteem and worthiness. I definitely had some *aha* moments. The self-love course helped me think more positively and *know* that I'd soon be starting my fund.

The energy I acquired coming out of that seminar helped me flourish in early 2013. In fact, the affirmations, along with the "VAKS" were the springboards to nudge me to actually get an investor on board (see Chapter 5).

VAKS stands for Visual, Auditory, Kinesthetic and Spirit. Visual means doing an affirmation while moving. Auditory means doing an affirmation while listening and massaging your earlobes (one recommendation). Kinesthetic means doing a physical exercise (crossing your arms over your knees is suggested). Spirit means getting in touch with your soul (putting your hands over your heart while doing the affirmation is advised).

Affirmations are carefully constructed statements, said out loud or silently, which can transform your thoughts and ultimately your future. I find them more powerful when they are stated out loud. They are very useful, repetitive statements that should be charged with emotion. In short, items are more likely to manifest in your life quicker when repetition is used in conjunction with emotion, and not as a standalone strategy.

I started a new ritual: "Change your rituals, change your life."

I began saying my personal affirmations out loud every morning. Within a month, my two amazing daughters, Lauren and Morgan—at the time, aged seven and five—had memorized them. Doug Nelson, our teacher for most of the weekend, was one of the most dynamic speakers I had ever met. His book *Catch Fire: How to Ignite Your Own Economy* was another volume added to the plethora of books I read in 2011 and 2012.

Go to JoelSalomon.com (in the Manifesting section under Programs) to see the affirmations from the MMI course.

Among the brilliant and powerful quotes from Nelson during the weekend:

* "Financial freedom is being able to spend time (as much as you want) with the ones you love."
* "Your success in life depends on the size and quality of your network."
* "Financial freedom is spiritual."
* "You should be asking yourself: 'How do I make that passive?'"
* "Failure is the classroom for success!"
* "Until you stop caring what other people think, you won't be wealthy."

Two key messages from MMI were, "**Hesitation = pain**" and "**Act as if it were impossible to fail**" (from Dorothea Brande).

So, did I make a big mistake? I thought we would have all the money we needed when I walked into my new office in December 2012 and yet a few weeks later we didn't have *any* investors.

I asked myself this question many times over the coming weeks. But I knew this felt right. I knew I was *supposed* to start a hedge fund. I just didn't know where the money was going to come from.

So, I just went on working to reach my goals, without giving up.

Chapter 5

●　●　●

Can We Raise *Any* Money?

"To Know and Not to Do is Not to Know"

—LEO BUSCAGLIA

Despite *knowing* that I was supposed to be a hedge fund manager, I still had doubts. What did I learn in the first nine months of 2013? I learned to "Doubt the doubt." I learned to "Act as if." I learned to "Never give up." And I learned to trust my intuition.

If anyone had asked me in 2012 when I would start investing my LPs (limited partners) money, I would have said at the start of 2013. I went about the process of "acting as if," inspired by Dorothea Brande, who said, "To guarantee success, act as if it were impossible to fail." Even to the point of moving into new offices in Midtown Manhattan which my prime broker sub-let to my new firm, SaLaurMor Capital. I had my computer set up and worked with SNL to get access to start analyzing insurers. I spoke to former colleagues and even hired one

I had worked with at FSI, despite not having any money to invest yet. Sean Ryan helped me analyze all the banks and specialty finance companies that we might consider investing in.

The main part of my job in late 2012 and early 2013, was working with potential investors to sign on the dotted line and get them to become investors in this new start-up. Plenty of insurers were intrigued with our unique single-sector focus, but no one wanted to be the guinea pig.

January 2013 was spent meeting with insurers, fund of funds (alternative vehicles that invest in other hedge funds), and other potential investors.

January 25th was the first step in what I believed would be a long, rewarding relationship with an insurance company. I had a very good feeling after the meeting.

My counterpart said to me, "Joel, we are really impressed with your thorough process of analyzing insurance companies. And your past performance at Citi, especially during the credit crisis, was excellent."

He promised he would bring all the information to the ultimate decision-maker, the Chief Financial Officer of the insurer, in the following weeks.

Stay Tuned!

On February 11th, I had an excellent meeting with another institutional investor who said they were likely to invest in my hedge fund.

I felt like I was on the cusp of a dream that I had dreamt over and over again for so many years. I felt blissful.

So now we waited until we had a follow-up meeting in the next few weeks to iron out the details, including the exact amount of the investment and how it would be structured.

February is one of my favorite months of the year. And I realize that when I am happy, more things come into my life to be happy about. February is the month that both Lauren and Morgan were born. For many years now, they have been blessed with multiple birthday parties. One from their Mom, one from me, one from their school and another from their grandparents. At my house, they share their birthday celebration.

I greatly appreciate the miracle of life. The birth of a child should be well-celebrated. I often think back to their actual birth and re-member the miracle. From one tiny microscopic cell to more than eight pounds at birth. From there, how quickly the accomplishments start piling up. From eating on their own to being potty trained, from riding their bike to skiing, all the way to singing and acting in front of hundreds of people.

All of it makes me realize how grateful I am to have had children.

It's early March 2013 and without an investor committing to give us money to manage, I continued to "act as if." That is, I worked *as if* we already had the money in our accounts. What did I do? On my dad's birthday, I interviewed a woman for the position of my trust-ed partner, my Chief Financial Officer (CFO) and Chief Operating Officer (COO). She would be responsible for working with all of our service providers: our lawyer, accountant, fund administrator, compliance firm and prime broker.

Essentially, she was hired to make sure the operations ran smoothly and financial statements were accurate so that I could spend my time doing what I love. That is, analyzing companies, meeting with them and investing in them, along with being of service to others. And of course, some days watching their stock prices gyrate wildly. Surprisingly, I found out at the end of the interview that she was also a Pisces. She was interviewing on her birthday, March 11th.

I hired Anat to start a few weeks later!

March 15th is a milestone day. No, not for the insurance company to give us money to invest, but for them to get approval from their investment committee for a $10 million investment to be managed by SaLaurMor Capital.

March 25th really was our milestone day. We received the long-awaited email saying that our prospective investor was committing to the investment. I was indeed launching a hedge fund after all. All this work trying to raise capital had finally paid off.

All the acting *as if* seemed to become *it is*.

As Esther Hicks says, "There is nothing that makes you know your worthiness more than having something you asked for, actually delivered to you."

Now the real work began.

My newly hired CFO/COO and I started working with my lawyer to draft a term sheet that both sides could agree upon.

In addition to agreeing to this investment, this company decided to "seed" us. That is, they arranged to help pay for many of our expenses in exchange for becoming a part-owner in the company. This alleviated my worries about having to dig deep into my personal savings to fund the business—at least for the next two to three years.

Still, by the end of March, a final agreement was not in writing and we had agreed to meet again in April to sign the official "term sheet." Hopefully, our expert law team could complete the term sheet by that time.

I entered the second quarter of 2013 wondering when I could finally invest these funds.

What was going on in my head at this time?

Well, I had committed to spending a lot of money! I was paying monthly rent for the commercial real estate space. My lawyer and his partners were working hourly on the term sheet. Readers may know that New York hedge fund lawyers are not inexpensive. And of course, I was paying for the SNL database out of my personal savings. And no money was actually coming in.

"Paying yourself first"? Well, I continued to transfer money into my Financial Freedom Account every month, but "freedom" seemed anything but likely at this time.

Imagine you are me! What are you feeling and thinking?

I started worrying about credit card bills, child support, and monthly mortgage payments. My cash flow was indeed flowing, just not *in*!

How did I manage my money during these lean times? Well, I did what I recommend to my current clients. Skimp where you can.

People tend to waste so much money on a daily basis. Do you really "need" to buy a Starbucks latte for five dollars a day or could you have the coffee at your office? Do you have to buy lunch in midtown Manhattan and spend $12 a day, or could you make lunch and save $10? Can you eat breakfast at home instead of grabbing that bagel and orange juice from the cart on Park Avenue and spending $4?

Maybe you can go without cable for a few months and save $150 or more per month. Instead, you could stream Netflix or other online movies for a fraction of the cost.

See, right there you just saved $4,500! Invest that $4,500 a year over twenty years at a conservative 8% and you have over $260,000! You're well on your way to financial freedom!

Those who interacted with me during those early months of 2013 probably did not recognize me. I was tense and uptight. Though I continued to "Act As If" we already had the money and were investing it, I had considerable doubt in the solitary moments before going to sleep.

So, I "doubted the doubt." Why is the doubt right? Why is my fear of not succeeding correct?

So, I continued to *act as if,* and what happened? All of a sudden we had three strong leads. If we could get them all of them to invest, my incoming CFO believed that would be enough for SaLaurMor to be sustainable for a number of years. This was so exciting.

Our first "seed" investor had given us comments on the term sheet, and because of my naiveté I still believed we could get the funds invested within the month. But with the initial back-and-forth of our lawyers and their lawyers, it became clear that this may take a few weeks—perhaps months.

Yet I was hopeful to get invested in May. Sean and I started preparing a mock portfolio to track *as if* we were invested starting May 1.

We worked diligently on our stock ideas, along with meeting companies and doing our standard due diligence meetings and calls (contacting those companies that we were interested in investing in) with many of our top ideas.

I also went out to meet and talk to our pipeline of insurers. Two in particular seemed quite interested in investing amounts between $5 million and $10 million. The big question was, would they invest in May so we could finally stop running a mock portfolio, and actually be able to take advantage of some really cheap insurance securities next month?

The first few months in 2013 were quite stressful for me.

Though I was really close to realizing my dream, we kept on hitting snags in the process of getting the actual money from investors.

I was taking massive action and not seeing results. I began to get impatient.

The irony in that did not escape me.

I would ask my daughters whenever we got stuck in traffic or were waiting in a long line, "What are you learning, Lauren?" She would invariably answer "Patience, Dad."

"Morgan, what are we learning?" "Patience, Dad!"

Along with a lack of patience, I was also deficient in exercise and happiness.

I vividly remember a meeting in April 2013. A few portfolio managers and insurance analysts were there, and I happily heard one of the analysts talking about being overweight.

Misery loves company.

I realized I needed to lose weight, and soon. I weighed more than I had ever weighed in my life.

Being competitive and goal oriented, I challenged the analyst to a weight loss contest. The contest should allow me to lose all the weight. Everyone in the room looked at me and laughed when I said I could lose more weight than my weight-loss opponent because if you looked at me you would not have guessed I was even fifteen pounds overweight.

Why was I overweight?

Because since I moved into my prime broker's space in December 2012, I was focused on getting the business up and running. I neglected my body. I was either analyzing the next stock idea, trying to raise capital through meetings with potential investors, or spending time with Lauren and Morgan. I had stopped exercising. Most nights I was going out networking. That meant calorie-rich hors d'oeuvres and alcohol. I was not eating healthy. And instead of jogging every weekend and several times a week, I was not jogging at all (See Appendix 3 for the full story of the contest I had in the spring of 2013 to lose the weight, and the techniques I used).

An interesting thing happened as I lost the weight, exercised more and ate healthy. I began to feel happier. I truly believe that exercise does benefit how you feel and improves your mental state.

I highly recommend reading *Healthy Brain, Happy Life* by Wendy Suzuki. The book provides a detailed look at how exercise impacts the brain.

Several studies show that moving your body for as little as ten minutes each day releases GABA (Gamma-Amino Butyric Acid), a neurotransmitter that makes your brain feel soothed and keeps you in control of your impulses. And so, as I became happier and enjoyed my life a lot more, additional positive items started coming into my life.

As the Dalia Lama says: *"our ultimate aim in seeking more wealth is a sense of satisfaction, of happiness. But the very basis of seeking more is a feeling of not having enough, a feeling of discontentment."*

We announced our second hire, after Sean Ryan, in May 2013 when Anat Leon became our CFO/COO and Chief Compliance Officer.

Our prime broker, Concept Capital (since purchased by Cowen and Company) assisted us in issuing a press release announcing her arrival to the world. One can't get enough publicity when you're a hedge fund trying to raise tens and hundreds of millions of dollars.

At the same time, I sent out a term sheet to another institutional investor.

I was excited that we could have two investors on board in just a few short weeks. I set up a call and we had a good discussion. However, the investor decided they were not interested in being a seed investor (or any kind of investor for that matter).

Yes, I was really disappointed. But I believed we were about to "launch" any day with the other investor's money. I also knew that there were many more insurance companies looking to improve their investment returns. There were at least a few others that were also prime investor prospects. In fact, I had a call scheduled with one— just a few weeks away—to discuss how much they would invest.

Additionally, I interviewed some top-notch insurance analyst candidates to work closely with myself and Sean. I was hopeful I could make a final decision in the next few weeks, around the time we would start investing the money.

Yet again, it looked like the investing wouldn't begin that month. Subscription documents had to be filled out. Those crucial documents give the fund administrator all the investor's information to help guard against fraud.

It's nearly summer. I am chomping at the bit to invest. Year to date, the market is already up almost 15% and I feel like we are totally missing out.

In fact, in my March monthly commentary written on April Fools' Day 2013, I entitled the piece, "What A Year." That's because the market had already jumped 14.5% in just three months (it was relatively flat over the following three). Worse, my favorite longs were moving up too fast.

I thought it would be interesting for readers to follow Phoenix Companies (PNX), a stock that we invested in at SaLaurMor, from 2012 through 2015, as we dealt with the volatility. I used it to explain our process, thoughts, and feelings. It should be enlightening for investors and non-investors, alike:

One example of "favorite longs moving up too fast" was Phoenix Companies (PNX). I had analyzed this company in late 2012 when it was $25.21 and saw the potential for incredible reward compared to the potential risk. My analysis showed a strong bull case scenario of $64.30 with a worst case scenario of $12. Clearly, this was a risky position, but the upside to downside was almost three times. Most stocks on my screen had less than two times and very few had the potential to double or almost triple!

For those interested in our general process on analyzing individual stocks, please see JoelSalomon.com (see the Investing Program and within that drop-down menu check out "Insights into the Investment Process").

As we waited for investors to give us the money to invest, PNX was performing quite well. As a non-investor, I would say "too well." In fact, by the end of May, it had already appreciated 67%. Nonetheless, my bull case scenario still showed more than 50% upside.

Before we began our investments, I decided to revisit all my "upsides to downsides" to see if they had changed because of the changes in interest rates and equity markets since the beginning of the year.

PNX's bull case valuation had indeed changed, as had its bear case. We found it was worth more than $75 in our bull case and just $25 in our bear case in early June. This implied that despite its 50% jump, the stock still had 78% upside and about 40% downside—almost exactly 2:1 upside-to-downside—with the highest potential price appreciation of all insurers we followed, except one or two.

Any professional, and a lot of individual investors, knows that emotions can drive dramatic market moves in the short term. The first five months of 2013 were clearly emotionally charged, filled with more greed than fear. As a result, stocks appeared to be more than fairly valued at that time.

I continued to play the waiting game in early June 2013.

Imagine how you would feel if you were on the cusp of a dream you have had, but it kept on being a little bit out of grasp. You are extending your arm to touch it but it is just out of your reach. You're stretching that arm as far as possible—a foot, two feet, even three feet—but you just keep missing it by inches. This is how I was feeling in early June. And yet, I continued to *act as if* we already had the money.

How did I do this?

What actions did I take?

Well, I spent many hours writing up analyses of companies. And Sean and I continued to work on a mock portfolio *as if* we were already invested as of June 1.

We even had daily morning meetings to discuss our top ideas. I would ask Sean, "Why should we buy this bank today?" And he would respond with his detailed analysis of the bank and his expectations for earnings and capital for the next few years. Then I would pepper him with questions:

"Why is this bank a better investment than Citi?"

"How will XYZ perform if the 10-year Treasury note jumps 1% next month or if it declines that much?"

"How sensitive is XYZ to the regulatory environment?"

"Is it an acquisition target?"

… and on and on…

I had learned from my time at Citi the importance of diversification. I remembered some excellent ideas I'd had both on the long and short side, and I was eager to express these views.

So when I had started at Citi in January 2008, I was all set to invest. I implemented my two top investments and my two top short ideas. Unfortunately, one of my shorts, a mortgage-related investment, jumped 20% in just a few weeks before ultimately falling more than 90% from that level later in the year. Because of my lack of diversification, this jump caused a hefty loss for a neophyte investor (me!)—not just in money, but in many sleepless nights.

So, I knew it was best to have a full portfolio of names numbering more than just four. In fact, we were ready in June 2013 to invest in more than fifty names. If one went 20% against us, the worst-case scenario was a loss of 1%.

As I waited for our investor (and our respective lawyers) to finalize the documents required to begin what I had waited almost twenty years to do, we monitored the mock portfolio movements on a daily basis. While I am not a short-term investor, it was interesting to consider the true volatility of a portfolio compared to what the historical market volatility (beta) was.

It is June 12th 2013! I was sitting at the Axis Capital Holdings Limited (AXS) investor day, half-listening to the senior management commentary, *believing* that today would be the day we actually received confirmation so we could actually invest the funds. Late that afternoon, we did indeed get confirmation that the funds had been received in the accounts and were available to be invested.

So, it's been twenty years since I had this vision. Twenty years! I wanted to align my hobby of picking stocks and my career. I wanted to align my passion for analyzing companies, helping others, and getting paid to do it. I wanted to align my passion for picking under- or over-valued securities and my job. And now I am actually doing it for real. It's the evening of June 12th and I can't sleep at all. Not because of fear but because of excitement. I am so excited to take advantage of the lucrative opportunities the world has to offer!

There had been so many twists and turns along the way! But getting the experience at Moody's and Swiss Re on the credit analysis side was so important. Of course, getting the actual portfolio management experience at Citi was essential. This, despite many investors who were looking to invest in my hedge fund, yet unwilling to give me credit for excellent performance in my more than three years there—during what some consider the most difficult years to manage money this generation has seen.

I had already decided to invest the large majority of the funds over a three-day business period, and keep some dry powder in case any of our favorite ideas incurred some significant price changes over the coming weeks. It turned out to be a good plan. We also decided to start the fund slightly short. That was because many of our top names over the last two to three months had moved very close to, or just above, our fair value estimates, which were for year-end 2014 or year-end 2015.

In my investor letter for June called "We have Lift-Off," I spoke of the start of my fund:

> … *Though we have discussed one lift-off, the more important launch in June—to us, at least—was the institutional one of SaLaurMor Capital as the first investor committed capital. Additional investors are teed up for the coming months. We wanted to thank our initial investors for their confidence and trust in us and remind prospective investors of our Founders Share class available in 2013.*"

The start of the fund was clearly exciting as you probably felt in the last paragraph. However, putting all the money to work cost the fund a lot in commissions and despite being "correctly" positioned (meaning we started slightly short and the overall market declined), we still lost money in our first partial month of operation. However, I was quite confident that our top ideas were the right ones for not just a few weeks—but for many months and indeed years.

> *"When you feel good, you naturally begin thinking empowering thoughts and saying things that uplift you; you automatically become magnetic to your dreams."*
>
> —SANDY FORSTER

It's July 2013.

Wow! I'm managing a hedge fund! My dream job had been realized!

The fun of getting up in the morning and no one telling you what to do, and coming home at night with still no one telling you what to do, except maybe a relative or child, was so enjoyable. I was so grateful to be doing what I love and to be able to find mispriced securities.

The volatility (changes in the stock prices) was quite high these first few weeks. I was *lucky*, for lack of a better word, to have had the experience from 2008 and 2009 at Citigroup to learn to weather these storms without giving in to panic. I had learned to be *mindful*.

What is the best way to handle a portfolio when the movements of stocks become extraordinary?

The simple explanation is to reduce your exposure. For example, if you are managing $24 million in stocks and $1 million in cash, increase your cash position to $5 million and reduce your stock position to $20 million.

What also tends to happen in periods of volatility is that large hedge funds require their portfolio managers to reduce their gross exposure, which means sell their long positions and cover (buy back) their short positions. This has the effect of increasing the overall stock market volatility even further, and creates what many in the business describe as a "risk-off" scenario. This was what was going on in late June and early July of 2013 across the market.

Until it wasn't!

As Kyle Bass stated in Tony Robbins' enlightening book, *Money: Master the Game*, "It's really how you deal with failure that defines you as a person."

To be sure, my first few weeks of managing a hedge fund might not have been deemed a failure. But for me personally, it was definitely not a success. Not being able to make money when we had the direction of the market right for the first few weeks, and then also not being able to make much when financials were the darlings of the stock market in July, was clearly not helping my mindset. It also didn't help that one of my highest conviction ideas dropped 15% in the first two weeks of opening the fund. Fortunately, the strategy of diversifying the portfolio from day one kept that decline from being too damaging.

Ultimately, the stock, which was a top holding, did rebound in July. And by the end of the month it had risen more than 20% above our cost. Without question, the market can make you very humble in the short term.

In the monthly commentaries you can find at JoelSalomon.com, every three months we discussed quarterly earnings with our existing and potential investors.

As long-term investors, we rarely saw the true economic fair value of an enterprise change significantly in any one quarter, yet the stock price movements seemed to be highly exaggerated. Many hedge funds "play" quarterly earnings events because of the large movements in stock prices.

I tend to believe that the movements are much more about sentiment and setup than changes in the true value of the enterprise. Setup means that if the large majority of investors really dislike the stock, and if the company reports good earnings or even in-line profitability compared with average earnings expectations, the stock price is likely to jump. Conversely, if the large majority of investors really love the stock, and if the company reports a bad quarter (below the average earnings expectations of sell-side analysts), then the stock is likely to collapse.

> *"It is not a case of choosing those [faces] that, to the best of one's judgment, are really the prettiest, nor even those that average opinion genuinely thinks the prettiest. We have reached the third degree where we devote our intelligences to anticipating what average opinion expects the average*

opinion to be. And there are some, I believe, who
practice the fourth, fifth and higher degrees."

—JOHN MAYNARD KEYNES, GENERAL THEORY OF
EMPLOYMENT, INTEREST AND MONEY, 1936.

Year in and year out, at least based on my few years of experience working at FSI and Citigroup, August seemed to be a month in which stocks dropped a lot.

Perhaps it is because I remember too vividly August 2011. That was when I witnessed a 14% collapse in less than two weeks after Standard and Poor's (S&P) downgraded the U.S. Government's debt securities to AA+ from AAA.

But a longer view of history shows that August is not even close to the two worst months of the year. September and May hold the dubious honors. On average, over the last 78 years, stocks have dropped 1.1% and 0.2%, respectively, according to S&P and Haver Analytics.

There is also the perception, which tends to equal reality in many cases, that professional investors head to the beach during those months and don't watch their portfolios very closely. As such, they are likely to sell in early August. Thus, they don't have to sell (or short) if anything unusual happens when they are on the water (out of the office).

In this day and age when portfolio managers have access to stock prices twenty-four seven on their smartphones and mobile devices in real time, it seems a dubious reason to sell. Yet, a lot of volatility continues to occur in August (see the August monthly commentaries on JoelSalomon.com).

2013 was a year in which those perceptions truly equaled reality. Many fears that investors harbored to make them sell before their vacations were well founded.

I, for one, held on. I wasn't at the beach.

August is, however, one of the few times during the year I spend some quality time with Lauren and Morgan. This year, 2013, we visited Pennsylvania amusement parks and their grandparents came along. Stops included Dutch Wonderland, Hersheypark and even a quick visit to the Amish Country.

At Dutch Wonderland, we just happened to be visiting at the same time as the sister of my oldest and dearest friend, Rob Davidsen. Her name is Nancy, and she, her husband and her son joined us for a fun day of rides and sun. I am grateful I had this time for a little R&R with my two beloved children and my parents. Thank you all for your support.

Here is what I wrote on September 3, 2013 about August:

"After seven months of relative complacency, investors were spooked in August, first by the apparent imminence of Fed tapering starting "too soon," given the recent economic data being generally weaker than hoped, and the "saber-rattling" of Washington D.C. to the atrocities in Syria.

As we penned back in early April (see our March 2013 monthly commentary at joelsalomon.com), complacency was rampant just a few months back despite the long list of potential concerns. Now, apparently, many of them are weighing on the market and financial securities, in particular, giving those with some intestinal fortitude the opportunity to buy relatively cheap.

August Review

August was the worst month for the stock market since May 2012 with the S&P 500 down 3.1% and the Russell 2000 slumping 3.2%. Financials fared even worse, down 5.1%!

We attribute most of this to profit-taking after the huge run-up through July, since the interest rate action—up another 16 basis points in August—continued to favor asset-sensitive investments."

Lauren & Morgan with the author and his parents, along with Kevin & Nancy Quinn and their son.

"Stress is not all bad"

—Wendy Suzuki

As noted, September *really* is the worst month of the year statistically for stock investors. 2013, though, was an exception to this rule.

The stock market, as measured by the S&P 500, exhibited what we deemed "short-termism."

After the VIX, known as the "fear index," hit a multi-month high in August, those fears quickly receded in September.

Maybe for some folks, it was getting the kids back to school (second and fourth grade already for my daughters). Or maybe it was the reality that many securities had become quite cheap. Whatever the reason, September of 2013 was a great month to be a financials investor. In fact, it might have been one of the best months for me as a portfolio manager. And not just because I was invited to see one of the all-time Yankee greats (Mariano Rivera, see below) being celebrated at Yankee Stadium just days from my birthday. The performance of the fund was gratifying after many months of what I personally viewed as weak results.

Mariano Rivera's last game at Yankee Stadium in 2013

"It's when you finally accept and feel grateful for your life as it is, when you no longer feel emotionally obsessed with your desire, that you finally detach. And in that moment, behind the scenes, your life turns around."

—SANDY FORSTER

As we entered another quarterly earnings season, as per usual, it was a time we tended to underperform because we devoted much more effort to analyzing long-term drivers of value than to divining short-term fluctuations in sentiment (as discussed above). I was being pushed by my colleagues and prime broker to spend more time raising money for SaLaurMor Capital.

Though it had only been four months since we launched, our returns were quite good but we hadn't raised another dime since the original investment. The pipeline of potential investors we had so diligently worked on growing in the last quarter of 2012 and the first half of 2013 was not as strong as it had been earlier in the year.

Why you might ask?

Well, I had spent my time focusing on investing and learning more about the companies we had already invested in or were considering putting into the portfolio. I *really* enjoyed this part of the job. The marketing part, going to cocktail parties, meeting new people, begging for money, was not something I relished.

We had spent time interviewing other firms to do this part of the job, but many of them required a retainer. As a small fund, we just did not have that in our budget. We did discuss hiring someone internally, but that person would have to be willing to get paid mostly based on future income and discretionary bonuses. This was usually a nonstarter for many marketers. So, we decided to hold off on hiring and I continued to do the two full-time "jobs" for the foreseeable future.

Looking back on the first nine months of 2013, it was a bit of a blur. But a pleasant, awesome blur! Yes, we had raised the money to get the fund going and we had actually started investing. And we had actually started making money investing. I hadn't given up. I did "doubt the doubt" and "acted as if" we already had the money. Everything was working fairly smoothly, though of course, more investors and money was necessary to keep the fund afloat for the long term.

Chapter 6

• • •

Relationships

In this chapter, I focus on a new romantic relationship. I realized that being in a relationship because you want someone else to make you happy is definitely the wrong reason to be in a relationship. Though we got along easily most of the time, I realized that despite my age, I was not ready for a real loving relationship because I didn't love myself completely.

As Esther Hicks says, "Mate with Your Soul."

After three really solid months of performance, both relative and absolute, I was feeling quite self-confident and my self-esteem was solid. Unfortunately, I was aware that my personal life was wanting as I was spending my free time either with Lauren and Morgan, trying to find new investors, or analyzing existing companies in the portfolio or potential new investments.

Being mindful means being aware of your own personality and your improvement opportunities. It also means just enjoying the little things in life, from the taste of your favorite food to the smell of a daffodil.

I have found that, though I had grown spiritually, in 2013 at least, I still wanted to be in a relationship to feel fulfilled and "worthy" and "wanted." Clearly, this is not the reason to search for a relationship. But I did. And, being in a generally happy and positive state, I attracted women who were also there.

In October, I began dating Debbie (for privacy reasons, this is not her real name). She was easy-going, fun, quick to smile and laugh, and it didn't hurt that she was also attractive. When we went back to her apartment, she had Post-it notes on her cabinets with inspirational quotes and sayings. I loved it! In fact, I had been putting affirmations on my cabinets since 2012 when I had come back from the MMI conference with Doug Nelson.

She had quotes from Earl Nightingale ("You become what you think about most of the time."), and Socrates ("I cannot teach anybody anything. I can only make them think. To find yourself, think for yourself."), and many others. My favorite was from *The Sermon on the Mount* which I happened to have up in my kitchen as well:

"Ask and it shall be given; Seek and ye shall find; Knock and it will be opened unto you. For everyone who seeketh, findeth, and to those who knock, it shall be opened."

Finally, she even had the affirmation from *The Magic of Thinking Big*:

[YOUR NAME] meet [YOUR NAME]: an important, really important person. [YOUR NAME] is a big thinker, so think big. Think big about everything. You've got plenty of ability to do a first-class job, so do a first-class job. [YOUR NAME], you believe in Happiness, Progress, and Prosperity. So talk only Happiness; talk only Progress; talk only Prosperity. You have lots of drive [YOUR NAME], lots of drive. So, put that drive to work. Nothing can stop you [YOUR NAME], nothing. You are enthusiastic! Let your enthusiasm show. You look good [YOUR NAME], and you feel good. Stay that way. [YOUR NAME], you were a great gal [guy] yesterday, you're going to be an even greater gal [guy] today. Now go to it [YOUR NAME]. Go forward!

I decided to copy her and put it up on my mirror in my bathroom a few months later.

The beginning of November was spent dealing with the normal quarterly earnings season traditions.

What are those you might ask?

Every quarter, publicly traded companies release reports detailing how much money they made in the previous three months, and investors at funds like ours compare those results to their models (spreadsheets used to estimate or "model" future profits) to determine whether the companies met, beat, or fell short of expectations.

Most companies also host conference calls to discuss their results with investors.

At SaLaurMor Capital, we took notes on the calls and sent them around to our colleagues. We also highlighted the positive and negative aspects on the calls. We discussed whether the call and the earnings report changed our view of the company's long-term prospects and if we should buy, hold, or sell (or sell short) the stock based on this information. Rarely did the new information change our view, but some part of the valuation might have changed.

As noted earlier, quarterly earnings seasons tend to be times of the year when we underperform. The volatility also picks up in individual securities as new information gets assimilated into stock prices.

November was also a month in which one of the aforementioned stocks jumped—the Phoenix Companies (PNX). In November, it rose 43% (!!). What changed in November compared to July through October when the stock was down slightly (about 7%)? Well, PNX was one of the life insurers most sensitive to changes in interest rates. Because of its high asset leverage (for every dollar of equity it had more than fifteen dollars of assets), it was among the most sensitive to small moves in interest rates. In November of 2013, the yield on the 10-year Treasury note jumped 20 basis points to 2.90%—equal to the high for the year. PNX was also very "equity-market"-sensitive, meaning that when the overall stock market went up, its value also appreciated. In November, the S&P 500 was up 2.8% after leaping 4.5% in October and 3.0% in September. These jumps, along with the benefit to PNX of higher interest rates, were slowly being reflected in its stock price.

Debbie and I spent the weekends when I didn't have Lauren and Morgan, getting to know each other. We went out for drinks and eventually dinner. I learned how kind and sweet she was. Also, though she was working at a University as an assistant, she had big dreams to become a film producer and even had the film all figured out in her head. She was smart and funny.

But I found that fitting in a blossoming relationship was a bit difficult. I actually craved getting to work on the weekends when I didn't have my daughters (as I had been doing since late December of 2012). I itched to analyze that next company, send out emails to prospective investors, write the monthly commentary—or all three!

In late November and early December, I decided that I wasn't comfortable not working at all during the weekends.

The key questions I asked myself were:

Is this because I didn't really enjoy my time with Debbie?

Or was SaLaurMor just more important?

I had spent most of my past relationships being a people pleaser. Some may say it's an admirable trait to have, but when you're doing it to prove your worth because you have feelings of inadequacy inside you, you shouldn't be doing it at all. I had also spent past relationships pretending or hiding how I truly felt and "going along for the ride" many times. I decided to express my true feelings in this relationship, and in December of 2013, I spent every Sunday working.

Six months had really flown by.

It's hard to believe I had been struggling to find an investor less than twelve months ago in late 2012. Back then I was working so hard to meet with potential investors and trying to find at least one that would commit to invest with SaLaurMor.

Now, we had received an institutional investor's money and we were investing it. I was spending my days analyzing securities, meeting companies, and investing in them. Though the job was humbling many days, it was also fulfilling to see some top ideas really working. Knowing that the stock market misprices securities—and sometimes by a very wide margin—was encouraging.

However, the list of securities was getting slimmer and slimmer because the market had an amazing amount of appreciation in 2013.

As I later detailed in my investor letter from January 2014:

"In 2013, the S&P 500 index was higher by 29.6%. The Russell 2000 small capitalization index leapt 37%, the financials index we follow jumped 33.4%, and the Hennessee long/short equity index was up a very solid 17% (just through November). In a year when the average insurer in the S&P index was 47% higher and life insurance companies accelerated 63-67%—depending on your favorite measure—investors were rewarded for bearing market risk."

I had come to realize how macro-driven the life insurance and regional bank space was. This means the broad economic factors which at times impact many stocks at once and include interest rates, currencies, commodities, and the overall stock market itself.

The correlations between different stocks were very high (we wrote about this extensively in the first few monthlies—see JoelSalomon.com).

Many times, these whole sectors were moving almost as one, making life difficult for a fund like ours which seeks to pick the best (and worst) individual stocks.

Still, I was hopeful that as we ended 2013 with spectacular returns for the stock market—and in particular financial stocks—the outperformance of financials would continue into 2014.

However, as a credit analyst by training, I remained skeptical.

In fact, we were positioned this way with an overall stock market hedge as part of our short book. This implied we were making an implicit bet that financial stocks would significantly outperform all other sectors of the market, going forward.

In December, I enjoyed my first real vacation with Lauren and Morgan since the fund was started. We traveled to Florida to visit Walt Disney World and Universal Studios. My cousin, Ira Trager, and his daughter, Michelle, joined us this year. The trip was a much needed refresher for me.

It is always good to get away from the cold and dark Northeast U.S. and enjoy warm weather in December. It was also good to get away from watching the minute-by-minute ticks of security prices. It brings perspective, which is absolutely necessary in the business of investing.

The Phoenix Companies (PNX) stock increased another 3.5% in December, ending the year at almost exactly $60. Remember my initial analysis had pegged the bull case scenario at $64.30, and I had adjusted that to $75.00 in June of 2013 after the improvement in new money rates and equity market in the first five months of 2013. I was loath to increase my bull case further despite the company's sensitivity to these factors.

We ended 2013 with excellent performance and exceeded even my lofty expectations. In just over six months of operations, SaLaurMor Capital was up about 10%, and as I noted in the investment letter written on January 6th of 2014:

> "With about six months of track record, we are quite pleased that total alpha generation [how good you are at stock picking] is approaching 800 bps."

Debbie and I spent New Year's Eve in New York City. I had done very little planning for what many consider the biggest date night of the year. We had a special dinner at a great seafood restaurant on the Upper West Side of Manhattan, but it was too early to spend the midnight hour there, and they had another round of guests coming in anyway. So we left and spent the first minutes of 2014 at a local tavern. It wasn't ideal, but I rationalized at least we had the time together. I actually had arrived back from Florida just a few hours earlier with Lauren and Morgan. It was a whirlwind day, and staying up a few minutes past midnight was sufficient for me to christen the beginning of my first full calendar year as a hedge fund manager.

Happy New Year!

Or is it?

The huge run that financial stocks and insurers enjoyed in 2013 came to a quick halt in January 2014.

Though we were a true hedge fund taking little market risk, the downdraft in financials was so significant that we barely outperformed the stock market. Correlations, which I noted in December seemed to be increasing, went sky-high in January. My lack of confidence and doubt grew daily. Stock ideas I thought were still misvalued—many by more than 20%—dropped more than 10% in January.

Happily, our existing investors did not call asking what was going on. Yet the only thing potential new investors wanted to know about in January was how we were doing amid this carnage. My "canned" answer of "we are not short-term investors and I don't look at the 'P&L (profit and loss)' daily" was not what a new investor wanted to hear.

PNX was an example of the wild moves in January of 2014. With the yield on the 10-year Treasury note collapsing more than 30 basis points and the stock market itself down over 4%, PNX shareholders were not happy. In fact, in just three short weeks (well, actually they were the longest of my career), the stock was back to where we had bought it in June at about $42—down about 30%!

Here is one case where our stop loss criteria (see Investments under the Programs drop-down menu at JoelSalomon.com for a detailed discussion on stop losses) worked well and we sold most of the security with less than a 25% loss. We were looking smart as the stock continued to weaken and fell below $40 in mid-2014. Stay tuned!

I did a lot of introspection in January and February of 2014, our first back-to-back losing months. I went back to some of Doug Nelson's inspirational quotes from MMI from December of 2012. I needed a good reboot to get back to *believing* in myself and my top ideas.

* Business as usual is not good enough!
* You are making what you do because that is what you settle for.
* Unless your life is on the line, you never give it 100%.
* Act like your life depended on it, all the time!
* What is stopping you from making more?
* What we know that just ain't so is our greatest obstacle!
* The first step in learning is awareness!
* Confidence is so important in success.
* You need to be willing to get uncomfortable.
* I am a generous giver and an excellent receiver.
* Lucrative opportunities always come my way.

"The Key to Every Man is His Thought"

—RALPH WALDO EMERSON

So we became more aggressive in raising capital for the fund. It had been nine months since we launched. While the returns were not spectacular, and less than I had hoped for when I decided to pursue my dream job, they were worth marketing. We started working with our prime broker to set up meetings with potential hedge fund marketers. We could hire employees or outsource the marketing to a third party. In February 2014, I spent more time marketing—going out and talking to potential investors about SaLaurMor Capital. I even got invited to a few capital introduction meetings which were set up by our prime broker, Concept Capital.

In the hedge fund business, capital introduction is when potential investors and hedge funds meet to discuss if the investor would like to invest money in the hedge fund. Many times these meetings are like a speed-dating event. The investor moves from table-to-table, meeting with multiple hedge fund companies with different strategies, and the hedge fund meets with multiple types of investors.

At one event, I met with a family office, an insurance company, a small college endowment fund, and multiple fund of funds. A family office is a private wealth management firm that serves ultra-high net worth investors. Fund of funds are investors that invest in multiple hedge funds to diversify their risks for their investors who tend to be high net worth individuals.

I had to make another important decision in early January. The signup for the Association of Insurance Financial Analysts conference (AIFA, *pronounced* "A"-FA), which would be starting March 1st in Boca Raton, Florida was due. To get a hotel room, I really needed to make a reservation in January. And though my relationship with Debbie was going okay, she was clearly much more excited about it than I was. The source of conflict was that we weren't spending enough time together.

Should I invite her to AIFA?

We'd been dating for less than three months. I did enjoy spending time with her but we had our differences. She wasn't really interested in exercising and I realized that I had to carry the conversation most nights. We did have a lot in common, though her knowledge of investments was quite limited.

I decided to put on my "people-pleasing" hat and asked her to come with me to AIFA. She agreed and we started talking about how it would work. I explained to her the logistics and how the first night I would most likely spend trying to chat with potential investors. And she obviously had no obligation to listen to me chat hedge fund-ese and insurance to executives of insurance companies. But we could get there a night early and have twenty-fours to enjoy the hotel and even a local bar and restaurant.

She became quite excited since she didn't travel much. For me, this was just another business trip and I knew we really wouldn't be spending much time together since I would have early-morning-to-evening meetings on Monday. And on Tuesday I would have a full day of meetings packed into just six hours, until we left Tuesday afternoon.

February was also the height of the quarterly earnings season for most financial stocks that we had invested in. This was already the third earnings season for SaLaurMor. As discussed, we spent a large amount of time listening to the earnings call commentary by the management teams of the companies we had invested in. We then tried to update our models as quickly as possible to see if there was indeed any change to our economic fair value estimates. Many times this happened in the following month or two or three.

Volatility of stocks tends to increase during earnings season, and that February was again no exception to this rule. We had one stock plummet over 15% that difficult month.

March 2014 was another month filled with marketing.

I began the month by going to the AIFA conference in Boca Raton. I figured I could kill two birds with one stone by researching my favorite insurance companies while also meeting with potential insurance company investors.

Many had still been talking about investing in a hedge fund in 2013, especially if an astute hedge fund manager listened carefully to their quarterly earnings calls. I met with a number of reinsurance companies and specialty insurance companies; the abundant cocktail hours and dinners were great places to talk to prospective investors.

I followed up throughout March, setting up meetings and calls with insurers later in the spring.

Debbie was not interested in spending time with insurance executives talking about premiums, soft markets, interest rates, macro factors and new regulations. But I used it as a great opportunity to describe our investment process and outlook for the industry over the near- and medium-term. I was able to pursue existing leads and add to our pipeline.

Debbie did allow me to put into perspective the importance of just working on getting new investors. We did spend most of Sunday by the pool. Though of course, I was reading quarterly reports and annual statements while she was reading a novel. I must admit I did jump in the pool as well. And on Saturday evening we enjoyed some fine local seafood before the conference began the next day. I even was able to get a jog in around Boca before we went to dinner on Saturday night.

Being mindful of your surroundings and appreciating the Boca Raton resort was important in the midst of a very intense—though fun—few days. I also was mindful of my relationship with Debbie and how, as the short trip went on, I was enjoying my time talking insurance at the cocktail parties and meeting with the insurers more than the short breaks to see her. I had asked her to Boca because I was being a people-pleaser and not because I was in love with her. Reflecting on those few days on the way back home made it clear to me that Debbie wasn't "the one." And that Tuesday night we had a long discussion concluding with the ending of the relationship.

So, what were my lessons learned from this relationship?

Stop being a people-pleaser!

Knowing that I am the most important person in my life and doing things for others when they don't feel good to me is not the way to live my life.

And if you are not in a place of true self-love and mindfulness, it will be really difficult to have a happy relationship with another.

Also, don't get into a relationship to heal your soul or to have someone make you happy. Only you can do that! And don't get into a relationship to feel fulfilled and "worthy" and "wanted." These are more terrible reasons to get into a relationship.

Chapter 7

● ● ●

Being Grateful

Gratitude is one of the most important feelings you can have. Esther Hicks says it is equivalent in energy and vibration to love and appreciation. Staying at the emotional level of grateful feelings is just awesome.

The law of attraction says, the more things you are grateful for and the more items you can recognize gratitude for, every day, the more experiences there will be that will come into your life to be grateful for.

Wouldn't you like to be counting your blessings all day long?

And they don't have to be Big Hairy Audacious ones (like the kind of goals Jim Collins talks about in *Built to Last*).

Tony Robbins asks:

"What can you be grateful for today? Who can you be grateful for today? Could you even be grateful for some of the problems and pain that you've been through in your life? What if you took on the new belief that everything in life happens for a reason and a purpose, and it serves you? What if you believed in your heart of hearts that life doesn't happen to you, it happens for you?"

I decided to write down what I am grateful for in a journal—a gratitude journal. It definitely made me feel better even though I still did not have enough investors in my hedge fund for it to be a long-term viable business.

I realized one can be grateful for many, many, many things in life.

I started with obvious items, such as good health, my daughters, and my parents. I quickly got a list that was several pages long. It included my friends, acquaintances and colleagues who had helped me get the hedge fund up and running. It included gratitude for having made money in 2008, and making a lot more in 2009 and 2010. And gratitude for supportive family members and for being able to do my dream job. And finally it included all the material possessions I currently had and those that were on their way.

"It's gratitude," Sir John Templeton replied to the question of "What is the secret to wealth?"

I realized I was grateful for being an actuary, a CFA, and all the knowledge I had acquired over the years.

I also realized I was grateful for having had the opportunity to do what I love. I was grateful for being my own boss.

I wrote down all the books, textbooks and leisure readings that I'd read over the years.

"Gratitude unlocks the fullness of life. It turns what we have into enough and more. Gratitude makes sense of our past, brings peace for today, and creates a vision for tomorrow."

—MELODY BEATTIE.

The most important aspect of the gratitude journal is the feeling of it. When you actually sense the amazing feeling of what you have, then the world is your oyster because isn't that what we are all after anyway—the feeling of bliss and happiness?

When I actually turn back time to the birth of my daughters and picture myself in the delivery room with Christine, seeing the miracle of child-birth, that is when I feel immense gratitude.

To feel the feeling of the miracle of life is what it is all about. If you can feel that feeling or an equivalent feeling in your life, then you are clearly more happy and blissful, enjoying life itself at that moment. And wouldn't it be great to feel *that* feeling as much as possible all day every day?

Following up with all the insurers I had met with at AIFA in March felt like a full-time job—unfortunately, a marketing job. I was also interviewing a number of potential marketers for positions at SaLaurMor.

I stopped feeling sorry for myself and went back to my feeling of gratitude. Shouldn't I be grateful I now had a pipeline of new insurers interested in investing in SaLaurMor?

An advertisement we placed in *Bloomberg* earlier in the year had really spurred interest. I give a lot of credit to my CFO/COO for handling all the interviewing. Her screening saved me at least fifty hours of time which would have been wasted on candidates we just couldn't afford to pay or were just not qualified to market our fund.

I realized how grateful I was to have a CFO/COO who saved me so much time and effort and allowed me to focus on what I enjoyed!

In April and May of 2014, I spent most weekends analyzing insurers. The list of write-ups we now had, numbered more than fifty. Updating the models was also very time-consuming, but it was interesting to see if our estimate of fair value had changed significantly after each new piece of information was added. Generally the answer was no, but the few times the estimate did change significantly helped generate some "alpha" for the fund. Alpha is the measure of a fund's return relative to its level of market risk.

I had also decided to re-invest in The Phoenix Companies (PNX) because it had languished in the low $40 range in May and our valuation range was still $25 to $75. Clearly, PNX did not have the same outsized potential reward to possible risk when we had originally "found" the idea, but it was still quite attractive compared to many other securities.

We also believed PNX would be an interesting acquisition target for many private equity investors or other domestic or international life insurers.

And we considered a price of $80-$90 to be reasonable given PNX's equity value at the time.

So, be grateful for even the little things, or be grateful for the incredible, awesome things. I recommend starting a gratitude journal (as I did in 2012).

Chapter 8

● ● ●

Happiness

*"We hold these truths to be self-evident, that all men
are created equal, that they are endowed by their
Creator with certain unalienable Rights, that among
these are Life, Liberty, and the pursuit of <u>Happiness</u>."*

—THE DECLARATION OF INDEPENDENCE.

Being happy is all in your control. Not the government; not the economy; not your neighbor, your spouse or your child. It is all in your control.

Once we *know* that, life can be so much easier.

Unfortunately in 2014, I definitely didn't *know* that.

I believed that the stock market and my stocks controlled my happiness. If my longs went up and my shorts went down, we made money! And boy was I happy. If my longs went down and my shorts went up, we lost money! And boy was I depressed!

My happiness was being controlled by physical reality. It was controlled by observing instead of creating happiness from within myself to know that everything would be just fine. It's a given that when you feel happy, more and more things come into your life to be happy about.

By doing things that made me happy to begin with, I knew I could make myself happy. I could listen to my favorite songs or spend more time with my loved ones. I could do things I loved, like exercising. analyzing a company or helping someone find a job. I could also say positive affirmations and declarations.

In *Man's Search for Meaning*, Frankl talks about happiness:

"But happiness cannot be pursued; it must ensue. One must have a reason to 'be happy.' Once the reason is found, however, one becomes happy automatically. As we see, a human being is not one in pursuit of happiness but rather in search of a reason to become happy."

Doing nice things for others also helped me.

As George Bernard Shaw said:

"People are always blaming their circumstances for what they are. I don't believe in circumstances. The people who get on in the world are the people who get up and look for the circumstances they want, and if they can't find them, make them."

I felt like not a lot was working in my portfolio. In fact, for most of the time during the first five months of 2014, I should have flipped the portfolio—been invested in the shorts and betting the longs would drop. This type of price action is usually because of "risk-off" action or "de-risking." When large hedge funds (and they represent the vast majority of trading on some days) are selling their longs and covering their shorts, the opposite of what should be happening, based on fundamentals, occurs. Cheap stocks get cheaper, and expensive stocks become still more expensive. This is what is known as a "risk-off" or "de-risking" period in the market.

A large hedge fund that specialized in financial stocks, laid off a few portfolio managers earlier in 2014. These multi-billion dollar portfolios were all unwound. Longs were sold and shorts were bought back in the first few months of 2014.

This caused a lot of the de-risking impact I experienced in the SaLaurMor portfolio.

All portfolio managers tend to believe they have unique portfolios. But of course, when I looked at the top investors in many of our largest positions, I found some well-known hedge funds including Citadel, Millenium, Och-Ziff, Omega, and Paulsen.

I spent a lot of time soul-searching in the first half of 2014.

I began trying to overcome large doubts I was having about my expertise as a portfolio manager and investor.

There are many ways to overcome negative energy (aka sadness). I started with listening to some favorite songs. One was

"Believe" by Nick Swisher, a former New York Yankee baseball player whom Lauren and Morgan and I had met when his album came out in 2011. Another was one I started listening to after the MMI in 2012, when Doug Nelson suggested picking a song to lift you up when you're down. I picked "I Believe I Can Fly" by R. Kelly.

The songs helped. But I probably should have been listening to them throughout the day, not just at 6:00 a.m. when I was brushing my teeth and shaving.

I also realized I wasn't enjoying what I was doing most days.

It hit me that I was not feeling happy getting up each day. I wasn't pursuing my "unalienable right."

I tried other ways to become happy.

It dawned on me that after so many money-losing days, I was almost expecting to have a losing day. I would wake up unhappy or worried. As Napoleon Hill said, "No man who fears anything is a free man."

As thoughts are indeed things, my vibrations (as Esther Hicks says in *Ask and It is Given*) were not in alignment with Source—God, Allah, Tao, Buddha, Jesus, or the Universe.

I knew I had to work on my feelings and my negative energy.

I also realized I was being fearful and not taking action.

Fear is really the opposite of faith. Fear is the belief that you are going to perform poorly or worse. Fear can be debilitating and even lead to death.

There is a famous story of the hazing done by university students back in the early 1900s. The freshmen were being initiated by the juniors and seniors. One freshman was blindfolded and brought to a train depot. There he was tied securely to the train tracks. Soon a train sounded its horn miles in the distance. The juniors and seniors left the young man explaining he had to get loose or he was going to get hit.

The upperclassmen had strapped the freshman to a track that was not in use, of course. But when they returned after the train had passed by on the other track, they found the freshman dead. Unable to get free, the young man was literally frightened to death.

His fear had stopped his heart!

Another powerful story about fear comes from Viktor Frankl. He tells in Man's *Search for Meaning* how he once had a conversation with a well-known composer who had confided in him that he'd had a strange dream.

The composer relayed how a voice told him that he could wish for anything and that he should only say what he wanted. Then, all his questions would be answered. So, he wished to end his suffering and be liberated so his misery would be ended. And Frankl asked, "When did you have this dream?" The composer answered he'd had it in

February 1945, and it was then early March. So, the composer asked when he would be liberated and the dream voice had answered March 30th. The war continued on and there was no good news. It appeared very unlikely that he would be freed by the end of the month. On March 29th, the composer became very ill, ran a high temperature and by the next day he was unconscious. On March 31st, he died!

Viktor believes that the close connection between the state of mind of this man and his courage and hope implied that the sudden loss of this hope and courage was deadly. His loss of hope led to his death!

I myself had many a fearful day during this period. There were some times when I had done the analysis, found what looked like a great stock idea, but was unable to make the investment—or—*take action*!

This happens to many portfolio managers but it is not talked about often. Living in fear is being scared of making a mistake and thus missing out on opportunities by not taking action. There were many days during the first half of 2014 when I failed to take advantage of mispriced stocks because of this fear.

Everyone can be hopeful or be fearful. I was clearly not hoping for the best. I was not hoping or believing that my top stock ideas were going to work—I was worried they wouldn't!

Some Lyrics from Nick Swisher's "Believe"

"Random acts of kindness happen all the time, but they mostly go unseen.

It's not always front page news when you do the right thing.

It'd be so much easier to walk away. Go about my business and live selfishly.

So when I start to get caught up in my own world.

Something stirs inside of me. I look in the eyes of an innocent child and that voice inside me starts to sing…"

Nick recommends having faith in your fellow man.

Try to be mindful and read the actual lyrics to "Believe" (You can listen to the lyrics at JoelSalomon.com under the "GET INSPIRED" tab and then the "SONG LYRICS" tab). They are powerful. I especially connect with the "random acts of kindness," which I began employing in my daily life. I truly *believe* that all things are indeed possible if you believe.

I remember listening to music even before I was a teenager and not really listening. In fact, the songs my fellow fifth graders and I were listening to had the best beats, not the best lyrics. And my daughters even now rarely listen to the lyrics of the words being sung. But being mindful in all your actions can be helpful in keeping you focused and becoming even happier.

Lyrics from "I Believe I Can Fly" by R. Kelly

"I used to think that I could not go on
And life was nothing but an awful song
But now I know the meaning of true love
…
If I can see it, then I can do it

If I just believe it, there's nothing to it…

If I can see it, then I can be it
If I just believe it, there's nothing to it"

I highly recommend reading the actual lyrics to "I Believe I Can Fly." I find the most powerful words are "If you can believe it, there's nothing to it." Most people wait to observe something before they can believe in it. To me, having faith is believing in the not yet observed—in things that have not yet happened. I learned to have a lot of faith in 2014. (You can listen to all the lyrics from "I Believe I Can Fly" at JoelSalomon.com under "GET INSPIRED" and then go to "SONG LYRICS").

June was a much better month for SaLaurMor. It was also a better time for me.

After practicing a lot of techniques to change my mindset, I felt more positive.

Besides the songs I was listening to, I started a process of saying positive affirmations and declarations.

The difference between an affirmation and a declaration can be minimal, but, significant.

Affirmations are positive statements asserting that a goal you wish to achieve is already happening. Sometimes the little voice in our head might say something like "No, that's not true." I now refer people to a quote from a conference I went to in December 2015: "Doubt the doubts."

A declaration is for stating a course of action.

Usually, a declaration is not saying that something is true. It is simply stating that we have an intention of doing something.

In June 2014, I also began Tapping, otherwise known as the Emotional Freedom Technique (EFT).

EFT is a form of psychological acupressure that is based on the same energy meridians that are used in traditional acupressure. Tapping utilizes the body's energy and stimulates points by tapping on them with your fingertips and literally "tapping" into your body's own energy and healing powers.

Paul Pompeo had become fascinated with this technique in early 2013. I joined him in a Sunday night ritual of participating in a webinar sponsored by Tony P., a friend of Paul's, known for his expertise in EFT. He suggested various techniques for eliminating negative energy. One common affirmation we did to shift energy was "Even though I have all these feelings of "X," I love, accept and forgive myself anyway."

True self-love, I found, is rare in most individuals. We must remind ourselves about being loving to ourselves on a daily basis.

I later read Wayne Dyer's outstanding self-help book, *Your Erroneous Zones,* which discussed areas of improvement for individuals, including not blaming others and making sure you don't live your life trying to please others. This book, written in 1976, was the number one best-selling book in the 1970s in the United States!

I actually started using EFT with Lauren earlier in 2014, when she had had trouble sleeping. We started a routine that shifted the energy. She had been taking 45-60 minutes to get to sleep, and many nights waking up in the middle of night needing comforting. With EFT, she went to sleep in less than twenty minutes, and often less than ten minutes. Plus, she rarely woke up in the middle of the night after we started using EFT.

Another remedy to shift my energy, was giving.

I found out how much better I felt when I was helping others. So I started a routine based on my readings from *How to be Wildly Wealthy Fast*.

Author Sandy Forster recommends doing five nice things a day.

It can be a simple act like holding the elevator for someone in your building, holding the door open when you enter a room, or saying "bless you" when someone sneezes. I found it easy to be nicer to others and that truly helped my mindset.

As Napoleon Hill stated in *The Master Key to Riches*, "We have never yet found a truly happy person who was not engaged in some form of service by which others were benefited. And we do know many who are wealthy in material things, but have not found happiness."

As I did more for others, I found opportunities to help others increased. On the weekends I didn't have my daughters with me, I would go into Manhattan to work and invariably see visitors from out of town using a map or clearly searching their smartphone for their next destination. This started happening so much I actually thought

I should invest in a firm that gave out maps throughout Manhattan like they do in foreign cities like Split in Croatia. Anyway, I was giving assistance and feeling good about helping others that were lost in the concrete jungle I call home.

I also saw more and more people needing assistance with their luggage as they entered or exited the subway. They were surprised to have a native New Yorker asking if they needed help lugging a suitcase up several flights of stairs.

In April and May, I wrote a piece titled "My Dream Job" for *The Actuary* magazine. The article was published in the June/July 2014 edition. I was surprised to see my article highlighted on the cover of the magazine!

I received a number of calls and emails from actuaries interested in learning more about my transition from working as a traditional actuary at New York Life to a hedge fund manager. Gladly, I met with a number of them and had very enriching telephone calls with others.

I explained to them how my belief and *knowing* that I would get to my current seat was what actually got me there. I did what Napoleon Hill stated in *Think and Grow Rich,* which was "Whatever the mind of man can conceive, and bring himself to believe, he can achieve."

Tony Robbins talks about giving in his life-changing book, *Money: Master the Game.*

"When giving outside of ourselves is done right, when it feels like a choice, when it connects us with others, and when it makes a clear impact, even small gifts can increase happiness, potentially stirring a domino effect of generosity."

Robbins also says this about giving:

"It primes our brain; it trains and conditions us to know that there's more than enough. And when our brain believes it, we experience it."

Robbins also quotes Sir John Templeton who said he didn't know anyone who had given 10% of what he earned to religious or charitable organizations over a ten-year period who didn't massively grow his financial wealth.

So, I began a giving program which was inspired by Paul Pompeo, back in 2012.

I handed out the book *Think and Grow Rich* to strangers, acquaintances and friends. I also found time to help people changing jobs or looking for jobs. We met for coffee or a drink. And I squeezed in some time to go to the New York Food Bank's warehouse to see their operations.

These little acts felt right and helped me get through some trying times. I remembered Sandy Forster saying that your life is a dream for billions of people around the world. If they could just switch places with you even for a day, it would be their dream come true.

• • •

Synchronicity is defined as "The coincidental occurrence of events and especially psychic events."

After being invited to a *Bloomberg* networking event in June 2014, which was the same night I had to be in Atlantic City for a capital introduction event sponsored by my prime broker, I had to make a decision.

I had planned on driving down to Atlantic City that night. The trip normally takes about two and a half hours, but with rush hour traffic it could take as much as four hours. I didn't want to leave later than 7:00 p.m. as I had early morning meetings with potential investors.

I mulled over the question—should I go to this *Bloomberg* event starting at 3:00 p.m. and ending with a cocktail hour starting at 7:00 p.m.?

The reason to go to these events is to meet potential investors or someone who knows investors. Those interactions occurred at the cocktail hour. I decided to go but would leave by 7:15 p.m. in case that typical drive to Atlantic City became a lengthy one.

I left the last presentation a few minutes early hoping someone would like to chat before the cocktail hour actually began. I met two individuals not likely to be investors, but who were good contacts.

I left the cocktail hour as most people were just starting to get their first drink. I was asking myself why I made all this effort to get to this event.

As I entered the elevator, I found my answer. I saw Pimm Fox! I had seen Fox interviewing panelists at many New York Society of Security Analyst Market Forecast Lunches (now known as CFA Society New York). Others know him as a *Bloomberg* Television anchor and radio host. I calmly said "Hello." He responded kindly, "Hi, how are you?"

Of course, I had not met Fox directly before.

As I left the elevator and walked out of the *Bloomberg* building, Fox walked the other way to Lexington Avenue. I thought to myself, wow, that was pretty cool having a nice brief interaction with him. But as I made my way to Lexington Avenue, I spotted Fox walking just ahead of me.

I caught up to him and asked him where he was going. He said he was walking home to his apartment on Fifty-Fourth Street and he asked me where I was going. I told him I was on my way back to my office at 1345 Sixth Avenue (between Fifty-Fourth and Fifty-Fifth Streets) to get my suitcase for my trip to Atlantic City. He asked why I was going there. I explained and he seemed quite interested.

I told him in our brief walk to Fifty-Fourth Street about my background.

I asked him if he ever needed a hedge fund manager to be a guest on his radio show. He said he did and he gave me his card. The next day I emailed him and through his producer we scheduled a visit for July.

Synchronicities!

I believe the real reason I went to that *Bloomberg* event was to meet Fox so that I could get some real exposure for investors to hear my top ideas.

"Of two or more competing theories, the simpler theory is most likely correct."

— Occam's Razor, circa *1348*

June 2014 marked the one year anniversary of SaLaurMor. Though the first six months of our one year track record had showed so much promise, the fund ended the first eleven and one-half months with less than 500 basis point (0.5%) of alpha generation (the measure of a fund's return relative to its level of market risk). In marketing the fund, this would not help our ability to persuade potential investors. The underperformance compared to what I had done at Citi and what I had expected was quite disappointing. I had been telling potential investors that we expected an annual relative return of 500-1000 basis points or 5-10% of alpha each year. Maybe this was to be expected though, given the performance of our sector.

Here's what I had written in my monthly commentary for May:

"As we approach our one year track record, SaLaurMor Capital has generated over 450 basis points of alpha, which is slightly below our annual target but not entirely surprising given the significant underperformance of insurers and financials in 2014 as noted above. Our net exposure to the life insurance sector this year has significantly hampered performance."

This was followed up with the following sentence in June:

"During the month, the fund generated over 200 bps of alpha. With a full year of track record, we are quite pleased that total alpha generation is over 700 bps."

June was clearly another comeback month for the fund after so many disappointing months to start 2014.

I was indeed pleased but still not ecstatic compared to where we had been after six months. And think about *this*:

"Past performance is no guarantee of future results."

I, like almost every investor, had expected an environment in 2013 that was almost nirvana for financial investors and insurance company speculators to continue. And yet for the next six months (and to foreshadow the future, indeed, for all of 2014) the exact opposite happened.

July 2014 was another month for quarterly earnings reports. More importantly, it was another month in which many of our top stock ideas had double-digit drops in just one month.

Year to date, the fund was down. Ugh!

However, in July, PNX had appreciated more than 11% and was getting closer to our fair value estimate. The upside was still more than 38%, making the stock one of the highest- appreciation potentials in the whole portfolio. So, we decided to continue to hold it.

I tried to be a long-term investor, knowing that many securities were being completely mis-valued. Still, the macroeconomic environment was the big driver of many of our top ideas. Interest rates drove almost all life insurers and regional banks' stock price performance despite the large disparity in their true sensitivity.

July was our worst month since January 2014. The month's decline felt worse following such an encouraging performance in June.

I realized that growth comes from adversity. And so far in my life, my biggest growth in terms of well-being, spirituality and goodness had come from the events in my life that had not been the most pleasant.

As Vic Johnson states in *Day by Day with James Allen*, "In our darkest hour it's hard to see the end of our circumstance. All we can think of is our conditions worsening. But it's usually at this time that our greatest growth can occur if we'll see the moment as a growth opportunity. If we'll see it as a time to learn how to control our thoughts toward an ideal that we cherish."

Vic quotes a poem he carries around. It is called "Don't Quit." I have also become very attached to it. I don't carry it around with me, but I do read it almost once a month:

"Don't Quit"

"When things go wrong as they sometimes will,
When the road you're trudging seems all uphill.
When the funds are low and the debts are high,
And you want to smile, but you have to sigh.

When care is pressing you down a bit,
Rest if you must, but don't you quit.

Life is queer with its twists and turns,
As everyone of us sometimes learns.
And many a fellow turns about,
When he might have won had he stuck it out.
Don't give up though the pace seems slow,
You may succeed with another blow.

Often the goal is nearer than
It seems to a faint and faltering man.
Often the struggler has given up,
When he might have captured the victor's cup.
And he learned too late when the night came down,
How close he was to the golden crown.

Success is failure turned inside out,
The silver tint of the clouds of doubt.
And you never can tell how close you are,
It may be near when it seems afar.
So stick to the fight when you're hardest hit,
It's when things seem worst that you mustn't quit."

July was a difficult month for us and trying to keep my faith was a struggle. But I practiced my new habits and started looking forward to another vacation in August with my daughters for a much-needed refresher. We enjoyed another week of amusement parks. This year we tried a park my oldest and dearest friend, Rob Davidsen, had recommended.

Knoebels in Elysburg, Pennsylvania is a large free-admission amusement park. It is renowned for its old wooden roller coaster called the Phoenix which was originally built in 1947. But the highlight of the trip was sure to be the motorboats and car rides that the girls love at Dutch Wonderland.

Before jumping ahead to this nice respite in August, I would like to note that one highlight for July was my radio appearance with Pimm Fox on the ninth. I talked about the background of SaLaurMor and two of my top stock ideas. The feedback was generally positive and Fox kept me on for two segments instead of just one. I received a call from a potential investor who listened to the radio broadcast and was intrigued with our investment process.

You never know…

> *"Your Attention, Please…Your Attention, Please…*
> *This… is the Universe. Today I'll be recording*
> *your every thought and emotion, no matter how*
> *"good" or "bad", no matter how generous or*
> *stingy, and no matter how helpful or hurtful*
> *they may be. And everything I record… will*
> *be played back for you, as soon as possible, as*
> *some type of physical manifestation in time and*
> *space. Thank you, that is all, The Universe"*
>
> —Notes from the Universe, Mike Dooley

August has historically been a good month for insurance investors. The reason is that many stocks are sensitive to catastrophes. Most of the property and casualty insurers, as well as reinsurers, tend to start outperforming other securities because the peak of catastrophe season is in early September. That's the real hurricane season, when a single storm can cause billions of dollars' worth of damage.

Remember the best month of my career was in August 2009, when both insurance securities and one business development company I held jumped. So, I generally have positive feelings and expectations going into August, and 2014 was no exception. Readers might want to go online now to JoelSalomon.com to read about an individual security called Fortegra Financial Corporation [FRF] which contributed to our excellent performance that month. You can find it under the dropdown for Programs in the Investing Section.

See how that works?

I felt happy. I felt positive! I expected good results and I received them.

I also enjoyed a nice respite with my daughters the last week in August visiting Dutch Wonderland and Knoebels. They did indeed enjoy the motorboats. I also remember quite vividly that old wooden roller coaster. Morgan loves to challenge herself and enjoys the thrill of a good roller coaster even more than her older sister. But the Phoenix was a bit too breathtaking, for even this eight year old. We got off, and all three of us agreed we were not going to do that again. The sound of the creaking was challenging, as were the hairpin turns! But we were all happy that we had "felt the fear and done it anyway."

I do remember having a really tough time leaving the park because of those motorboats. It must be a great feeling for a ten-year-old and eight-year-old to be in control of their own destiny driving around in one!

PNX was a very strong contributor to performance in August 2014. It appreciated 13% in the month (annualized, that would be more than 335%—or more than a triple!). Once again it was within 25% of our initial price target, but we decided to hold onto it despite now having more downside than upside.

> *"When in doubt, show up early. Think less. Feel more. Ask once. Give thanks often. Expect the best. Appreciate Everything. Never give up. Make it fun. Lead. Invent. Regroup. Wink. Chill. Smile. And live as if your success was inevitable, and it will be. Happy global domination!"*
>
> — NOTES FROM THE UNIVERSE, MIKE DOOLEY

"Leaning long" in the hedge fund context means taking more market risk by having more funds invested in securities that are held long versus held short. In September, that is usually the right course of action, especially with insurers. We stayed that course as another light catastrophe season passed.

However, September was another poor month for SaLaurMor and its top ideas. In the monthly commentary we wrote, four of ours dropped more than 7% in just one month! Our conviction level for these stocks was not diminished, yet our pocketbook certainly was.

PNX, though not one of our top ideas as it was at the time we had re-purchased it, also collapsed over 7% in September. Why? Well, one possible explanation is its relationship to the overall stock market index which was down 1.6% (it tended to go down more than the overall market and up more than the overall market). Another potential explanation is the delayed response to the collapse in the 10-year Treasury note. At the end of June, the note's rate was at 2.65%; by the end of August, the yield was just 2.46%. Clearly not helpful when PNX's earnings were dependent on the return on their assets, which were mostly corporate bonds whose yields were closely tied to the 10-year note.

My doubts about my overall ability began to creep back in. I felt like I needed more positive stimulus and began playing a new daily song.

I found some solace in Whitney Houston and Mariah Carey's "When You Believe".

Lyrics from "When You Believe"

"Now we are not afraid
Although we know there's much to fear
We were moving mountains
Long before we knew we could, whoa, yes

There can be miracles
When you believe
Though hope is frail
Its hard to kill…"

Written by Kenneth Babyface Edmonds, Stephen Lawrence Schwartz • Copyright © Universal Music Publishing Group

I urge you to go online and read all the lyrics to this beautiful song because—who knows what miracles you can really achieve when you believe? When you truly believe in yourself, somehow you will achieve. Readers can listen to the whole song at JoelSalomon.com.

So, all the techniques I was doing to be happier were helpful, but they were all external. The most important lesson from the first eight months of 2014 was: when I expected to be happy, I was.

When I expected "global domination," it happened. When I had fun, enjoyed myself and was being mindful with my daughters on vacation, then there were more and more experiences in my life that made me happy.

That is the law of attraction.

Chapter 9

• • •

Meditation

Why is meditation so beneficial for us? Quieting the mind actually opens us up to hearing what our inner being is telling us. It is that voice in our head; the sixth sense or intuition that is so powerful. And when we meditate, the whisper of the sixth sense may actually become a bit louder so we may hear it more often. I've found after years of meditating that I have started noticing nature more. And thus becoming more mindful. It allows me, as some of my friends have said, to be more "zen;" to not be so easily disturbed by the physical reality of the world around me.

Many will say "it's too hard." I recommend starting small, either with a guided meditation or just a few minutes a day. It is too important; start today. But don't just listen to me; read on for what some celebrities have to say!

Many intelligent and widely successful people recommend the benefits of meditation. Meditation has been advocated by the likes of Ray Dalio, founder of the largest hedge fund in the world, and Jerry

Seinfeld, comedian, actor, and star of the famous TV series that bears his name. Others who believe in its benefits include Oprah Winfrey, actors Clint Eastwood and Hugh Jackson, and Star Wars creator, George Lucas.

Dalio has said the power of meditation is in teaching the brain to maintain a calm, clearheaded state. Seinfeld said that meditation is a charger for your mind and body, just like you have a charger for your phone.

Tim Ferriss, author of *Tools of the Titans*, *The 4-Hour Workweek*, and many other books, recommends listening to one of your favorite uplifting songs in the morning and just sitting comfortably in a chair (he sits in a half-lotus position). Alternative methods he recommends are guided meditations by Sam Harris or Tara Brach. I personally use a guided meditation app called Calm, which I started using in 2016. I really enjoy the "Loving Kindness" guided meditation, but there are probably twenty or thirty you can choose from.

I remember a colleague at Moody's Investors Service practicing meditation in the mid-1990s after lunch. I recall catching her multiple times "snoozing" in the early afternoon. It took me years to realize how far ahead of her time she was.

Dr. Frederickson, a psychologist at the University of North Carolina, demonstrated the extent to which we can generate positive emotions from even everyday activities. She found that six weeks of training in a form of meditation focused on kindness and compassion caused an increase in positive emotions and socialization, and even improved function of one of the main nerves controlling heart rate.

I started with a CD series called *"Wings Unfurled"* by Lorna Byrne. A woman from my Mastermind Alliance in 2013 had suggested reading Lorna Byrne's book, *"Angels In My Hair."*

Lorna and I met in November 2013 when she came to New York City. The *"Wings Unfurled"* CD set was a guided meditation which I found very useful for calming my thoughts and mind. It allowed me to relax while the volatility of the stock market and our portfolio was not calm at all. I usually did the meditation commuting into Manhattan on Metro North in the morning on the 6:48 a.m. train. Using headphones after showing the conductor my ticket, I could be focused on her words for a good twenty minutes. Though many Monday mornings were actually spent sleeping for some of those minutes, I did notice life changes.

As I started meditating more often, I was able to appreciate more of life's little things I was typically ignoring. I became more mindful!

I started smelling flowers outside my building on Sixth Avenue. I lifted my face to the sun shining and would sit down to enjoy a beautiful sunset. And I became an astute people watcher.

There is no "right" way to meditate. I'd recommend starting either with just a few minutes a day—four to six at most—or with a guided meditation, where someone is talking you through at least a portion of it. And then, try to increase your daily meditation to fifteen to twenty minutes.

For many people in the finance industry and beyond, it is hard for them to shut their thoughts down for even a few minutes, and many have given up too quickly.

The real purpose of meditation is to quiet the mind so that you feel different in your body. Ideally doing it at home—not on the train or the bus—in the morning is best. As Esther Hicks says: "When you quiet your mind, your inner being works for you."

That is when you'll receive a thought. And your beliefs that are working for you won't change, but those that are working against you will.

Of course, the best type of meditation is one where there is no guide. That means you are just listening to your breath and not hearing any noises. Doing this for just a few minutes and eventually building up to fifteen or twenty minutes is likely to bring you significantly positive results.

Try it! Don't give up, and if you expect massive positive change, you'll get it.

I also continued to use Tapping (EFT) and I added a quick finger tap. This involved tapping your fingers together (first your thumb and index finger, then your thumb and middle finger, and so on) while saying some positive affirmations. This is useful in a public place where you are apt to feel uncomfortable tapping your head and face, underarm, and chest.

I was also working diligently on feeling good in the moment and trying to feel a little bit better than I was just the moment before. If I was upset about something, it was helpful to know that only I can make myself feel a certain way. No one else has the power over me to make me feel upset, angry or sad. Only I have that power.

Once I realized that and I was able to detach from the perceived importance of a particular stock or bunch of stocks, I felt much better.

I also spent a fun weekend with my daughters in September visiting Great Wolf Lodge in the Pocono Mountains of Pennsylvania. It was a quick trip but another reminder to live every day. Visiting in September is a bit more fun than in the colder months because of the outdoor activities they have added, especially the Howler's Peak Rope Course. Lauren and Morgan love the waterpark, and as they have gotten older they have pushed themselves to go on more of the waterslides. 2014 was the first year they tried the steeper slides. They certainly "felt the fear, and did it anyway." They now spend the majority of their time going on the steep slides when we go to the waterpark. I realized I should take after them more, or at least take more courageous action each day.

"Shoot for the Moon. Even if you miss,
you will land among the stars"

—LES BROWN

Maintaining excellent relative performance is what we hoped for when I started the fund.

The goal was to have small negative, or even slight positive returns when the market was down a lot, and positive returns in all up markets. Since we deemed ourselves a true hedge fund—meaning we were taking only a small amount of market risk—we didn't expect to outperform in strong bull markets (if the market was up 20% or more).

But it was comforting to a passionate investor and *believer* in market inefficiencies that sometimes the market would go down (sometimes a lot) and the fund could still make money.

This was what happened in October 2014.

The stock market collapsed almost exactly 10% from mid-September to mid-October, and the fund actually had a positive return during that period. However, the market rebounded so strongly during the next two weeks that looking only at the number for the month of October was very misleading. The S&P 500 was actually *up* 2.3% for the month, while the fund was up a similar 2.2%.

Despite not discussing the amount of time I had spent marketing the fund these last six months, it had taken up a large part of my time outside of the typical 9:30 a.m. - 4:00 p.m. trading day.

Most of my evenings had been filled with networking events where I met with high-net worth individuals and companies that might have an interest in a non-correlated market fund.

Correlation of assets is defined as the measure of how much investments move in relation to one another, and when. When assets move in the same direction at the same time, they are considered to be positively correlated. When one asset tends to move up and the other down, the two assets are considered to be negatively correlated. The correlation number spans from negative one to positive one or -100% to +100%.

SaLaurMor Capital was a fund that tried to limit its correlation to the overall stock market. So the goal was to have the correlation be close to "0," or, "non-correlated."

I had been interviewed on *Forbes.com* three times this year because of a "chance encounter." I really don't believe in chance. I do believe that everything happens for a reason and there are no coincidences, just synchronicities. I met a Forbes.com journalist at a New York Society of Security Analysts holiday party for a reason. The reason was to get SaLaurMor more exposure to a wider audience of investors so I could help more people.

The first interview of 2014 had more than 15,000 hits. November 2014 marked my third interview and it had received the second most hits of all the interviews I'd had so far.

This month I spent at least twenty percent of my *weekends* trying to reach potential investors via email and phone. I was also researching potential investors on *Bloomberg*, while researching companies that we were investing in.

Trying to balance the marketing side and the investing side of the business was, I believe, one of the most challenging parts of being a hedge fund manager. I had an internal debate with myself most weekends. Should I continue to analyze this financial statement or stop for the next hour or two and send out emails to prospective investors?

There was no right answer, but my true passion usually won out.

Doing what I enjoyed was essential to my successful months like August 2014. Meditating helped me be a more mindful money manager. Tapping also helped, but the key was "feeling good now." And doing my passion—analyzing stocks while helping others—was truly an awesome feeling. I realized I wanted to feel like that all the time because it made me happy. Meditation became a daily practice because it allowed me to "feel good now."

Chapter 10

* * *

Stop Losses, Stock Options, and High Conviction Ideas

Ask any two professional investors about stop losses and you are bound to get two widely divergent answers. Stop losses are trade orders in which the trader sets a specified price in order to limit his or her loss.

My own view is drawn from my own experience.

In 2008, while working for Citi, my analyst and I both had a high level of conviction on one of our largest positions. It tumbled in 2008 from $70 to $63, and then to $55 before the Lehman bankruptcy and AIG bail-out. Still, we held on.

In September of 2008, it dropped another 15% before rebounding a bit. Ultimately, we lost almost 65% on this one position when we finally sold it. Long-term holders brave enough to hold on or simply feeling it was not worth it to sell, however, enjoyed a 30% gain from 2008 through 2015.

If we had employed stop losses, which we began using at Citi in 2010, this significant loss would not have happened. Experiences like this led to SaLaurMor establishing guiding principles.

November 2014 was an example of using our strict guidelines for stop losses at SaLaurMor.

Our guidelines were simple—sell 50% of the position if we lost 15% from the cost of the stock, and sell the other 50% if we lost 25% from cost.

Early on the morning of November 6th, we realized our first stop loss (where we would sell 50% of the position) because of the 15% percent loss. We decided to sell the entire position in the stock at slightly more than $10. Two years later, the stock was still more than 50% below where we sold it.

This is a situation where taking emotion out of the decision was quite beneficial.

Clearly, I had to take action anyway while being upset and angry at myself for making the original decision to invest in this security, and ultimately making it one of our biggest positions. Having the stop loss criteria in place required me to sell half the security by the end of the day, or at the latest, the next morning.

The pressure was off on making that decision, but I did decide to make another important one that day on timing. We sold the *whole* position before 10:00 a.m. that morning at an average sale price 15% higher than where the stock closed that day. The next day it was another 3% lower. The day after that, it had sunk 17% at the low. The stock did rebound somewhat in the weeks following. But as mentioned, it was still more than 50% lower over two years later.

For those looking for more information on stop losses and the reasons I sold this security in particular, please go to the Investing section under Programs on JoelSalomon.com.

At SaLaurMor, we restricted our use of options to hedging and the overall use of options was quite rare.

I had learned a great lesson from my time at Citi regarding options.

When I started at Citi in early 2008, I had very high conviction about one particular short idea. The main risk to any short is the possibility that the company is acquired, since it can cause the price to spike overnight. At the time, this security was trading in the low $60s and I thought the risk of an acquisition was low. However, my manager recommended talking to the derivative specialist at Citi just to see if there was a low-cost way to hedge this risk.

We had a great discussion. I became much more knowledgeable about options after my colleague explained to me that we could buy a call option, sell a put option, and not have to spend any money!

My big mistake here was setting the price too high for the strike price of the put option. I figured the security we were shorting was worth $40 in our "downside risk" scenario. So, our derivative specialist told us we could sell the same total dollar amount of puts at a $40 strike price to offset the cost of us buying those calls at $95.

Great, no cost outlay and we are covered in almost all scenarios, right?

Well, as many investors may remember, 2008 was not the best year for stocks. Our great short idea dropped from around $60 to much lower than $40, and our short was hedged perfectly with the puts we had sold. So for every dollar the stock went below $40, we did not make any money, while the call option expired worthless.

I learned a valuable lesson about options, but also about fear.

We obviously could have just left the short position on without hedging the risk of it being acquired and made a lot more money. But we were fearful about the company being acquired. We had conviction in our top idea, but we didn't have absolute faith. Though we did have faith in the quality of our research.

Again, I clearly learned some valuable lessons about options, but also about having high conviction in your ideas.

For those interested in a detailed discussion of stock options and my experience in particular, please go online to JoelSalomon.com in the Investing section under Programs.

Chapter 11

● ● ●

Overcoming Feelings of Lack

With most of 2014 complete and the fund being down for the year, I had significant feelings of "lack." Again my happiness was conditional. If we were making money, then I was happy. If we were losing money, then I was sad.

And then the follow-on feeling was that I was not abundant; that I didn't have plenty of money for the rest of my life. Overcoming this feeling was my goal for the end of 2014.

PNX rebounded a bit in October and November and was essentially back to the level at which it was at in late August of 2014—about $61, still 23% away from our target price. This happened as the 10-year Treasury note stabilized (albeit at 2.3%, down almost 70 basis points from its recent high in December 2013) and the overall stock market continued to stampede to new bull market highs. In fact, the S&P 500 was up about 5% in those two months, much better than the overall financial index or life insurers.

It's December, so it must be time for a trip. This year we went to Great Wolf Lodge, again, in the Pocono Mountains of Pennsylvania. This was our first trip to the Lodge during the week-long winter break. In the prior four years, we had gone to Walt Disney World and Universal Studios.

Maybe it was partly because of the disappointing year-to-date performance of my hedge fund in 2014 or just me having doubts as to whether I could really afford another one of those big vacations (remember: "thoughts are things").

So, let's talk about lack; lack of money. I was feeling poor. As I teach my clients now, I had a poverty consciousness which clearly was ridiculous, but when you start feeling a certain way it is hard to shift yourself toward feelings of happiness, abundance and bliss.

Having not earned much money through the first eleven months of 2014, I was not feeling worthy, abundant or prosperous. Thus, my decision to vacation locally without the additional costs of flights, car rentals, and high-cost lunches at theme parks. Clearly, we could have afforded it, but my feelings of lack of money overcame that.

This is an easy feeling to overcome and I teach my clients how to shift their feelings of lack to feelings of abundance. I teach them how to be committed to saying money affirmations, listen to self-talks and shift limiting beliefs to empowering beliefs around money.

We were all programmed during childhood. Many of us were taught that rich people are evil; you can't be spiritual and rich, or Robin Hood was *just* in taking from the rich and giving to the poor. So, we have to be "reprogrammed." We have to be taught that we are worthy. We were all born with tremendous resources. And by shifting from fear to faith and saying certain words, we can become prosperity conscious.

But everything does happen for a reason. And what a great surprise it was to bump into an old friend at a place we had probably visited twelve times already. This is what I had to say about our trip to Great Wolf Lodge in the monthly commentary written in early January 2015:

"On a recent trip to a Pocono waterpark, the Salomon family bumped into a former reinsurance colleague. For those who have children under 15 (or remain kids into their 50s) and who enjoy waterslides, wading into a wave pool, and a 'lazy river,' Great Wolf Lodge (owned by well-known private equity firm, Apollo Global Management LLC [APO]) is probably quite familiar.

After the acquisition in 2012, APO has renovated the resort to include a bowling alley, miniature golf, and most recently, the Howlers' Peak Ropes Course, for those who have no fear of heights when walking 50 feet above the ground on a tightrope.

But for many children, the 'quest' is the highlight of the trip. In this game, the children—guided by many a parent in tow— roam around the hotel with a 'magic wand' looking for crystals, gold coins, words like 'courage' and 'commitment,' and people in trees or the 'man in the stump'.

During this adventure, my former colleague and I reminisced about our time at Swiss Re AG (SREN.VX)."

December would also end up being our best monthly performance since starting the fund. We benefited from owning Meadowbrook Insurance Group (MIG), a company I had known for over ten years because of the investment FSI made even before I arrived there in 2004. MIG jumped 39% in December mostly because Chinese firm, Fosun, announced its intention to acquire it.

We also benefited from the leap in PNX. Despite the decline in both interest rates and the overall market, the stock had its best month of the year, up 15%.

Now it was less than 10% from our price target. We decided to hold on. Why? That's a good question. If a stock got to within 10% of a price target, I would ask Sean, "Isn't that stock more of a short than a long now?"

However, sometimes when a stock is "working," the investor will tend to hold too long. Is it greed?

I tend to tell friends the famous Stanley Druckenmiller line is important to remember:

> "*The first thing I heard when I got in the business, not from my mentor, was bulls make money, bears make money and pigs get slaughtered. I'm here to tell you I was a pig. And I strongly believe the only way to make long-term returns in our business that are superior is by being a pig. I think diversification and all the stuff they're teaching at business school today is probably the most misguided concept everywhere.*"

So, I held on. Emotions can lead a stock to much higher values than are fundamentally justified as well.

Could PNX jump to $80 or $90? That was also something that ran through my thoughts in late 2014.

Other securities also helped performance that month. I'm not sure why we had such good performance after what had been a very, very tough year.

Maybe it was the time spent enjoying my daughters. Maybe it was focusing on feeling good right now. Maybe it was focusing on feeling just a little bit better than the moment before. Could it be because I was focusing on all the good in my life and being grateful?

I'm not sure, but it was a good feeling to be in alignment with all the good in the world.

December 2014 was also the release of the latest *Annie* Movie starring Jamie Foxx as Daddy Warbucks and Cameron Diaz as the wicked Miss Hannigan. Lauren, Morgan and I all loved the movie. Ten-year-old Oscar nominee, Quvenzhane Wallis stole the show. She sang "I Think I am Going to Like it Here," including what I *believe* is a line that every youngster and adult should say over and over again: "I think it and it appears." I also really enjoyed the songs "Opportunity" and "The City's Yours." They both had inspirational lyrics! From "Opportunity"," I loved the words: "Oh, I used to think what I wouldn't give for a moment like this. This moment, this gift! Oh, now look at me and this opportunity is standing right in front of me… my big opportunity. I won't waste it. I guarantee." The lyrics from "The City's Yours" that stayed with me were: "Anyone can make it, even you… in New York City."

My feelings of lack quickly subsided while I was having a fun week with my daughters and my former colleague and his family. They were replaced with feelings of abundance and prosperity and faith—faith that I was indeed a good money manager and faith that I was indeed worthy of all that there is available to me.

Though SaLaurMor Capital had a positive return in 2014, it underperformed the small stock index and the insurance index slightly. But because of our low exposure to the market, our benefit from stock picking was only slightly negative. Despite all the ups and downs of 2014, we were still able to make money for our investors and our performance was consistent with the overall hedge fund index in 2014.

Chapter 12

● ● ●

To Lever or Not to Lever: That is the Question

"The man who acquires the ability to take full possession of his own mind may take possession of everything else to which he is fully entitled"

— ANDREW CARNEGIE

Another year already!

2015 was our third calendar year managing money for outside investors. We still had not received any additional capital from other investors, despite all the time I had spent marketing.

But we'd had numerous inquiries about setting up a "first loss" separately managed account into which I personally would put up my own money (as the first loss) and the investor would put up an additional investment equal to ten times my own investment. This would allow us to increase both assets under management, and our profitability.

It was something I was reluctant to do because of my lessons learned from the financial crisis about leverage. But I realized that if we didn't do something in the next year or so, the fund was unlikely to survive!

I was getting a lot of pressure from my colleagues to do this as well. And if I am perfectly honest with both you and myself here, it was mostly because of my "seeking approval" behavior that I was even considering doing this.

At the time, my intuition, a.k.a my sixth sense, was screaming "*No!*"

Was it fear, or a sense of "knowing?"

At the time, I was not sure, but going with my intuition would have meant not even considering this extreme step.

Since a lot of my decisions in life were made to please others, I had this ingrained thought to consider others in any decision. And clearly this decision would be beneficial for my colleagues who were being underpaid and overworked.

But if I was truly "selfish" and only thought about myself in 2015, I would not have invested more of my own savings to get additional outside money, thereby creating even more *leverage*.

February rolled around again.

And another year to celebrate Morgan and Lauren's birthdays. Each year at my house, there had been a different theme. In 2014, *Frozen* was the popular movie and we had Dave's Cast of Characters, a local company specializing in entertainment for children's parties, bring in their *Frozen*-like princess character. In 2015, *Minions* was sure to be a hit after the movie *Despicable Me 2*. It was fitting that the birthday party for the girls had a *Minions* theme.

It was such a pleasure spending the time planning this event and then to have my daughters really enjoy their birthday celebration with friends and relatives. It definitely took my mind off stocks and made me realize how important the other things were in life—such as celebrating the birth of a child, a smile when they're happy, a contagious laugh, or an unprovoked hug and kiss.

Lauren and Morgan celebrating their 9th and 11th
birthdays with a Minion and friends.

The birthday cake for Lauren at her 11th birthday party.

The birthday cake for Morgan at her 9th birthday party

We've already discussed stop losses, and February 2015 was a month when we hit a stop loss in PNX. After hitting its peak in late December 2014 at just over $70, the stock proceeded to decline 18% before the end of February.

This was not in strict adherence to the stop loss principle since our actual guideline was based on the initial cost we purchased the stock at. But here I was using what investors call the "high water mark" or the recent high closing stock price for the stop loss percentage.

Thus, using this new, more conservative method, we had hit our first stop loss, therefore cutting our position in half in February.

"Do one thing every day that scares you"

—*Eleanor Roosevelt*

It was now March 2015 and I made the tough decision to go forward with the "first loss" separately managed account. The fund of funds also decided to give us additional capital on top of this investment, which would truly increase our assets under management dramatically. Now, we went about working with our legal team (and theirs) to iron out the details. I was hopeful that we would be able to put this money to work in the following month. Only time would tell.

We were still working with our counterparty to iron out the details of the separately managed account. I was a bit surprised it was taking this long, but we now "acted as if" again, and modeled this portfolio's attributes with specific stocks selected "as if" we were managing this money in April.

We were still hopeful we could invest the money in May, given all the good ideas we had at the time. The additional capital we were going to be investing in the separately managed account had still not been received as we ended April and approached the end of spring, however.

Though I still had second thoughts about this separately managed account, I invested anyway, knowing it could be a good source of income for SaLaurMor, albeit with potentially high risk.

April was also the month that we hit our second stop loss on PNX. After ending February down about 19% from its recent high-water mark, the stock collapsed in March to end the month down another 13%. This was a full 28.6% from its peak just a few months back.

After the dramatic drop on the last day in March, we decided to use the high-water mark stop-loss criteria and sell the remaining shares over the next few days. Ultimately, the loss from the high-water mark was over 30%, though this portion of our investment was about flat with our initial one back in June 2014.

What changed?

Well, the company had disclosed its first-quarter loss and its equity had weakened dramatically—effectively declining 22% in the quarter—because of a legal settlement charge and poor mortality (more people died than they had expected).

Though selling the stock at an average sale price in the $40s felt terribly painful, especially after having owned it at almost twenty dollars higher in December and January, it was this adherence to our stop-loss criteria that allowed us to actually make money on the position overall and avoid the catastrophic decline that soon followed.

In April, the stock was annihilated, down 28%. May was even worse, as speculators and shorts began to believe it could go out of business because of its weak capital position.

If April was annihilation, May was death; the stock plummeted 50%.

May 2015 marked the start of the new "first loss" fund investment as the paperwork was at last finalized. We had actually succeeded in getting a new investor, though it was in a separate account with lower fees. Part of the reason was our long-term relationship with the ultimate decision maker at this firm. The other reason was that I was investing some of my own net worth in the separate account. This amount would then be used to give us access to substantial additional investable funds. I was excited to put more money to work in many of the same stock ideas I had been investing in for the last two years. But we (well, I) made use of substantial *leverage*.

May was also the month I started listening to Bob Marley's "Three Little Birds," which is famous for the line "Every little thing is gonna be alright."

It so happened that one morning in May, Lauren and Morgan and I heard it on the radio.

The nights I had my daughters, I spend time with each one reading to me. This particular night in May, Lauren was reading a book of inspirational quotes that she had started in April. It was effectively a calendar of the year in quotes. I told her that particular Saturday night that she could read to June 18th (putting her about a month ahead of the actual date), which I figured would take about fifteen to twenty minutes. This way, she wouldn't be up beyond her 10:00 p.m. bedtime.

Much to my surprise, when we got to the last inspirational quote of the night (for June 18th), what did I see? Bob Marley's "Every little thing is gonna be alright."

Synchronicities seem to be happening more often in my life (and Lauren's).

"Don't worry about a thing
'Cause every little thing gonna be alright
Singing' don't worry about a thing
'Cause every little thing gonna be alright
Rise up this mornin'
Smiled with the risin' sun
Three little birds…"

Songwriter: Bob Marley

Three Little Birds lyrics © Kobalt Music Publishing Ltd.

It's June 2015 and we've been up and running for two years now. Time has really flown.

We've had many accomplishments over the twenty-four months. Lots of publicity, and in the hedge fund capital raising business, (almost) all publicity is good. We've gone to many conferences and presented our unique way of managing money.

The fund's performance, though, had been much worse than we had hoped for when we started in June 2013. Though June 2015 was our best month of the year, I had a strong feeling of foreboding. I was not sure why, but I had learned from the teachings of Esther Hicks that I should trust my gut and trust how I feel. Something didn't feel quite right and I wasn't sure what it was.

Sometimes it's hard to distinguish between a feeling of foreboding that's based on fear and doubt and a feeling that is truly based on intuition or your gut (your sixth sense). How can you *know* when you are acting out of fear and doubt rather than a feeling of intuition that something "bad" is going to happen?

My recommendation is: go back to meditating and try to really be mindful.

Is it a feeling that makes you feel scared or fearful? Or does this feeling make you feel empowered like you can take advantage of "all the lucrative opportunities the world has to offer"? If it is the former, the feeling is likely not intuition, but just a strong negative feeling which can be overcome by meditating or doing something that makes you happy (see Chapter 7: Happiness). However, if meditating doesn't change the feeling and you know you should take action to "take advantage of the opportunity," that is using your intuition.

I figured it out a few days later.

July 2015 was our worst month since we opened the fund for business in June of 2013. I knew why my stomach was in knots the last week or two in June and why I was feeling off and unable to sleep.

Being short many property and casualty insurers because of weakening fundamentals was clearly not the right investment decision for July. The proposed acquisition of Chubb Corporation (CB) by ACE Ltd. (ACE) had investors re-thinking the proper valuation for every property and casualty insurer—from those worth less than $1 billion, all the way up to companies worth more than $25 billion. It took us a few days to "reposition" the portfolio, but by then the damage had been done.

Leverage worked in our favor and despite having a bad month in July, we were not losing much money in the first few months of the separate account.

Chapter 13

●　●　●

Feel Good Now!

As my hedge fund performance was weak through the first seven months of 2015, I was again reacting to physical reality rather than creating my own future by feeling good. I continued to observe real life and not see what I wanted. I felt bad or sad or depressed based on how the portfolio performed.

Doubt had leapt (not crawled) into my mind and now took up a big part of my thinking. Did I make a terrible decision starting this company? We were down over 3% for the year and massively under-performing. More importantly, I was not feeling confident or happy doing my dream job.

I redoubled my efforts toward feeling better. One way was listening and singing to more inspirational songs in the morning as well as at night. I spent more time meditating and writing in my gratitude journal and trying to get my emotions right.

Also, I thought about other actions I could take to feel better *now*.

In addition to the songs, meditating and expressing gratitude, I did some brainstorming. Other items I added to my repertoire included more exercise. I found that jogging more or longer created a good feeling and I wanted to do it more. I also noticed that when I exercised to exhaustion, I felt the same way. I began pushing myself to do more pushups until I was completely spent.

I commenced doing EFT more, including during the day when I felt stressed or upset about a stock moving the wrong way. I usually went to the bathroom or walked outside to actually do the Tapping around the body. But also I would do the 'short-cut' tap using the finger-to-finger technique.

Then I tried other techniques:

1. Getting outside for thirty minutes a day to take in the sun's ultraviolet rays.
2. Doing more nice things for others. I went back to trying to do at least five nice actions per day.
3. Going dancing more. I had found that moving my body was therapeutic.
4. Reading more non-fiction books made me feel more positive. It helped me focus on what I could create and how I could change my circumstances.
5. Restarting the mastermind group that had gone fallow in 2014. I found that when you had like-minded people in a room, there was a synergistic effect that happened and I felt better after these meetings.
6. Finding things to laugh about. That usually happened on the days with my daughters since they can be quite silly and tend to laugh easily. Lauren, in particular, is a very good joke teller.

I also started watching funny movies or old comedies on television. In fact, we changed the TV station in our office from CNBC (and watching all news all the time—which was mostly negative) to cartoons!

Cathy Goodman tells her personal story in the book, *The Secret*:

"I was diagnosed with breast cancer. I truly believe in my heart, with my strong faith, that I was already healed. Each day I would say, 'Thank you for my healing.' On and on and on I went, 'Thank you for my healing.' I believed in my heart I was healed. I saw myself as if cancer was never in my body. One of the things I did to heal myself was to watch very funny movies. That's all we would do was just laugh, laugh, and laugh. We couldn't afford to put any stress in my life, because we knew stress was one of the worst things you can do while you're trying to heal yourself. From the time I was diagnosed to the time I was healed was approximately three months. And that's without any radiation or chemotherapy."

7. Forcing myself to smile even when the day wasn't going great. It is hard to cry or be depressed or upset when you are smiling. I also began saying to myself "I don't know why this is a good thing, but it will be. Everything tends to work out for the best in the end." Try it!

8. Hugging. Most people don't get enough tactile contact. We began hugging in the mastermind group when everyone arrived and when everyone left. A minimum of four hugs a day is recommended, and I definitely got at least that amount on

the Mondays when we had our meeting, and of course on Wednesdays, Thursdays, and the weekends when I saw my daughters.

I realized that I was feeling bad because I was focused on what I didn't want. I had to consciously shift my thoughts.

"JUST HAVE FUN!"

— *Joel Salomon*

After having a disastrous performance in July, I resigned myself to another subpar year, compared to my initial annual expectations. I realized that I wasn't savoring my experience. I was doing my dream job, but not really enjoying the day-to-day. The most important message I can give readers is to enjoy the journey because when you get there you might say, "Is that all there is?"

Consider your favorite ice cream flavor—the one you choose after tasting many—so that when you go to the best gelato shop in Venice or Rome, that flavor is what you order.

When you get your favorite ice cream in a cone or cup, what do you do?

Do you say "I'm going to see how fast I am going to finish this cone"?

No!

You savor it!

It's your favorite. It's the one you've been waiting for on that warm summer day. When the ice cream starts dripping down the cone you go crazy and make sure your tongue gets every little drop. If it drips on your arm, you even lick there, right? You enjoy every lick.

So, why don't we do the same in our life experiences? Where are we going anyway? Where are we rushing off to? The next meeting? Why not savor every moment? That is being mindful!

• • •

What was August for me?

It was time to focus on fun activities again. August is vacation season and in 2015 I made a big decision. Despite the challenges at the fund, I decided to take *two* weeks off: One to spend with my daughters again visiting Dutch Wonderland and Hersheypark. The other was my first vacation without my daughters since starting the fund. I decided to go to Croatia with my good friend, Don, a fellow financials stock investor.

I had decided not to take a flight from Rome back to New York on August 24th because my flight from Dubrovnik to Rome and the one from Rome to New York were only forty-five minutes apart. What if the Dubrovnik flight was even twenty minutes late?

So, I decided to spend the night of August 24th in Rome. I arrived in Rome at around 12:30 p.m. to be greeted by very large down moves in European insurance companies. Prompting the sell-off was China's decision to let the Yuan depreciate against the dollar by just 3%. The

S&P 500 futures market was trading down 4%, implying that this would be the worst day for the overall market since I opened the fund in June 2013.

When I got to my hotel, I had a big decision to make.

I hadn't been in Rome since 1999. It is one of my favorite cities in Europe and indeed the world. It is an open-air museum.

Should I spent the only day I have in Rome (and who knows when I will get back since it's been sixteen years!) in my hotel room watching stock prices drop (and maybe rebound) or should I go and visit the Roman Forum, the Coliseum and whatever else I can fit in during the few hours in one of my favorite cities in the world?

I decided to put in some trade orders (consistent with our strategy) in case some of our favorite longs dropped too much, and then I went to the Coliseum for a tour. This was almost exactly at the time the stock market opened.

Since I had opted not to have wireless service, I required WiFi to check stock prices. My signal was not the best at 9:35 a.m. Eastern Standard Time (EST).

There apparently was something of a "flash crash" when the stock market opened. Some securities, such as KKR & Company LP (KKR) and XL Group LTD. (XL), dropped more than 30% (!!) in just a few minutes, before quickly recovering more than 20%. Some of these irregular trades were canceled.

I went on my merry way as a long-term investor and enjoyed the guided tour of the Coliseum and its amazing history. I was being mindful and "feeling good now."

I then made my way to the Forum which I hadn't been to since 1999. I remembered all the historic treasures and, of course, the impact Julius Caesar had on the Forum.

But I made one silly mistake.

When I arrived at the Forum I found I had WiFi and I checked the stock prices of all of our positions as well as the overall market. I was quite surprised to see that almost every stock had rebounded from their opening swoon.

In fact, it was now almost noon EST (about 6:00 p.m. in Rome) and the market was almost flat! Not being close to the situation I felt a sinking feeling (that was fear and doubt!) that my short positions were going to hurt the portfolio dramatically if this rally continued,

I quickly called up my trader in New York and after several failed attempts (was the Universe sending me a signal that I misunderstood to *not* actually make these trades?), we were able to connect.

> Me: "John, cover our two largest life insurance company short positions!"

John: "What? Are you sure? Why?"

Me: "I don't know. It doesn't feel right."

John: "Okay"

I spent the rest of the evening at the Forum until it closed at 7:00 p.m. local time and made my way back to the hotel to freshen up for dinner.

By the time I had finished dinner and arrived back to my hotel, it was almost 4:00 p.m. EST. I checked the market and all the stocks we were invested in to see what had transpired in the last couple of hours.

I was once again surprised to see the market had collapsed *again*! And the prices of my favorite longs (and the few shorts I had bought back) had fallen back towards the lows of the early morning.

I realized that if I had just continued to focus on where I was and "be present" I would not have reacted to the morning rally. And I would have saved myself and investors some money. I sure wasn't practicing mindful money management!

As it was, the market closed near the lows of the day on August 24th of 2015, down about 4%. Our hedged portfolio had a disappointing day, down about 1%. Disappointing to me, because historically these were the days I had shined.

These were the days I had made money at Citi. So despite the massive outperformance of about 300 basis points, I was not happy. Being about 20% long meant that we should have been down only 80 basis points. Thus, we had negative individual stock performance that day—most likely from the few trades I had completed at the Roman Forum around noon.

And as one of my earliest bosses used to say, "Happiness equals reality divided by expectations."

A picture of the author with two "Roman soldiers" in Croatia

On August 25th, I had another important decision to make. I was on the 12:00 p.m. local time (6:00 a.m. EST) flight back to John F. Kennedy International Airport in New York from Leonardo da Vinci-Fiumicino Airport in Ciampino, Italy, near Rome.

I could buy WiFi for the flight and spend the eight hours trading from the plane or I could be a long-term investor and again put in some orders with limits and if they were hit then we would own (or sell) the securities.

I decided to get some much-needed reading in on the flight and not trade all day.

Everything happens for a reason!

When I landed, I saw what had happened to the stock market. In the pre-dawn hours of August 25th, it appeared that the market was going to rebound from the 4% decline it had the previous day. But it actually ended down about 1%. Before my flight took off and the market opened on August 25th, the futures market was indicating that the stock market was going to be up more than 2.5%.

So, when I landed, I found which trades had been executed. One big buy order hadn't been—by mistake. If I had bought the WiFi for the flight, I would have been communicating with my trader and we would have bought that security. And if we had bought that stock, we would have lost a lot of money since the stock apparently had fallen all day. And serendipitously, we were able to buy it in the post-market at a much better price and save investors a lot of money!

What did I learn from this experience?

First of all, being happy and following a clear plan, rather than just being purely emotional, really does improve performance.

August 2015 was our best relative performance month of any during my tenure at the helm of SaLaurMor Capital. The S&P 500 was down almost 7% that month and my hedge fund was up more than 3%.

Why?

I believe at least partly it had to do with being in a good state of mind.

We had also invested in Symetra Financial Corporation (SYA), which Sumitomo Life Insurance Company proposed to acquire in August for $32.50 or a 32% premium over the average stock price for the thirty days ending August 5th of 2015 (when SYA began trading with an acquisition premium).

We had invested in SYA in May of 2015 because of its significantly undervalued fundamentals and substantial excess capital position, along with its likely acquisition potential. It was one of just five life insurers under $10 billion in market capitalization which also had strong business fundamentals.

We had noted in our write-up dated May 26th of that year:

"We don't expect SYA to be acquired for similar multiples [to Protective Life], but at 14x our bull case 2016 earnings estimate, the stock would appreciate 27% [this equated to $30.9]."

Another key reason for our outperformance in August was our shorts. As I had noted in our investor letter:

"A number of shorts also declined dramatically more than the overall market, supporting the idea of being well hedged at all times. We had made some investments in companies that we deemed dramatically over-valued heading into August 2015,

and the market eventually agreed with us by the end of the month."

What did I do to be happy that month of August?

1. I was really enjoying myself: I took fifty percent of the month off on vacation. I was really enjoying the moment, especially while on vacation.
2. I was being present and not worrying about the future or the past. Enjoying life and focusing on the present actually is more profitable than worrying about what could happen. I was truly practicing Mindful Money Management. As I tell my daughters: "Worrying is negative future planning."
3. I was with people who were happy. Don is one of the calmest and best investors I know. He also was enjoying each moment in Dubrovnik and Split even with the volatile week of August 17th. My daughters were just having fun and enjoying the amusement parks, clearly oblivious to any stock market movements! It was this enjoyment and happiness that clearly rubbed off on me.
4. Lots of activity. I've talked about exercise in Chapter 5, but any activity is clearly beneficial and walking many miles each day around Split and Dubrovnik was especially healthy, as was walking many times around Hersheypark and Dutch Wonderland. I also had many swimming races with my daughters in the hotel pools.
5. It's ok to not be in control all the time. I realized that I didn't have to micro-manage every minute of every day and we could still make money. I took advantage of what I could control but I let go of what I could not.

6. Don't be so hard on yourself. Or putting it in the positive: love yourself for who you are. I started managing money in 2008 as being a perfectionist. I learned quickly how often you are wrong. Ted Williams (one of the best baseball hitters of all time) was, even in his best year, wrong about sixty percent of the time. Being a really great investor means being wrong about fifty percent of the time. I learned to love myself more and appreciate myself for who I was. I appreciated all my strengths as well as my improvement opportunities. Giving myself a break allowed me to enjoy being me more.

> *"The ultimate significance in life comes not from*
> *something external but from something internal.*
> *It comes from a sense of esteem for ourselves, which*
> *is not something we can ever get from someone*
> *else. People can tell you you're beautiful, smart,*
> *intelligent, the best, or they can tell you that you*
> *are the most horrible human being on earth—but*
> *what matters is what you think about yourself."*

> —Tony Robbins

Feeling good now and being mindful in my money management was mostly my experience in August 2015. Using all these new techniques to feel good now worked. But most importantly I realized that trusting my gut and not having to observe what was going on in the physical reality was huge!

Chapter 14

● ● ●

Trusting Your Gut and Unconditional Happiness

O nce again I had a feeling of foreboding.

Both August and September were very good months for the fund. August and September were both down months for the stock market, yet we were able to produce positive returns for investors.

Despite this, I was feeling off. But I didn't trust my intuition. Why not?

Remember Chapter 12, when I discussed the foreboding feeling in June of 2015? As I noted then, it is important to really figure out when you are feeling negative or have a feeling of something bad about to happen, whether it's an intuitive "hit" or just fear. When you start to use your intuition more and more until it becomes almost second nature, then you'll know you are acting based on your sixth sense and not based on fear or doubt. That is when you realize how powerful you indeed are!

And then there is happiness, which we've already talked about—but what about "unconditional happiness"?

Why can't we just be happy without any external events?

I think, like most people, we have been conditioned to only be happy as a function of external events. We observe our present situation and think, "Well, that's not good"—instead of *knowing* that it will get better. Once we *believe,* it will get better.

As I had noted in the investor letter, our fund generated over 3.5% (350 basis points) of alpha (positive stock selection) in September and produced a 1.5% return, while the market index dropped by 2.5% in the month.

The fund benefited from another investment acquisition. This time it was Amlin plc, a London-listed specialty insurer which we had invested in earlier in 2015. On September 8th, Mitsui Sumitomo proposed to buy Amlin for GBP3.5 billion or about 670 pence per share, which was a 36% premium to the closing price the day before.

Our investment in Amlin was, like SYA, based on our view of its huge discount to fair value. These types of investments tend to attract acquirers as well and we were not surprised that Mitsui made this offer.

Other reasons for the fund's significant outperformance in September included the reinsurers we had invested in. They not only rose in sympathy with the proposed Amlin acquisition but also because of the lack of major catastrophes in September as hurricane season passed its peak on September 10th. Actually, there had only been two major catastrophic wind events in October in the last twenty years—Hurricane Wilma in 2005 and "Superstorm" Sandy in 2012.

The fund would have had an exceptional performance in September if we had held on to the PNX stock we had sold in February and April.

On September 29th, Nassau Reinsurance Company announced its intent to acquire The Phoenix Companies for $37.50 for a 188% (!!) premium over the closing stock price of $13.03 on September 28th 2015. I received a number of calls and texts from friends and acquaintances asking me if I owned the security. I told them the story of our stop losses.

On the positive side, we had sold PNX at prices substantially higher than the actual acquisition price, and the high for September 29th was actually only $34.76.

Why?

Investors were skeptical that the transaction would be completed.

Nassau Reinsurance Company was unknown to most investors and they were adding $100 million to PNX's statutory surplus position which some speculators decided was not sufficient.

Furthermore, Nassau was a new company having only been launched in April 2015, and did not have long-term experience managing insurers. Thus, some speculators expected regulatory approval to be long and difficult (In fact, Nassau completed the transaction in less than nine months on June 20th of 2016).

Even without PNX, the fund was up 1.5% in September. I believe this type of outperformance was a result of many of the practices I had put into place earlier in 2015 which helped me remain calm while the market volatility was accelerating in August and September.

Still, something didn't feel quite right.

Not trusting these foreboding feelings was probably my biggest mistake in 2015.

Imagine an expensive wine glass just slipped out of your hand and is about to shatter into a thousand pieces. You know it is going to fall and break but just as it leaves your hand you see the result. And you can't do anything about it. This is how I felt in June of 2015 and again in late September of 2015.

Here I was enjoying an exceptional August and September, but not feeling quite right as September was ending.

My gut was telling me to listen to it. Over my many years of managing money, I've found my intuition to be quite sound. In fact, as I mentioned earlier, my experience has been that I tend to lose money or not make as much when I don't "trust my gut." And in late September my stomach was churning—making noises—again.

And it wasn't something I ate!

As I mentioned in Chapter 12, figuring out whether your feeling is truly an intuitive hit or a sense of fear or doubt is quite important. So it's helpful to go into a meditative state or ask yourself tough questions like:

"Why am I feeling this way?

"What is the worst thing that can happen?" Now back off from that worst-case scenario, since it likely has such a low probability of happening that it's not worth spending time on.

Doing these things can help you to decipher whether you are using your intuition or not.

• • •

In hindsight, without feeling particularly good or bad about an individual stock, it would have made sense to de-risk and sell longs while covering (buying back) shorts. But I didn't take that kind of extraordinary action.

Instead, here's what transpired:

I decided to add another song to my daily list. The girls had watched the movie *Descendants* and Lauren had told me about this great song "Believe." So I decided to start listening to that one too.

Here are the lyrics from Shawn Mendes' *"Believe"* from the Disney movie *Descendants*:

"I believe, I believe, I believe, hey...

Everest is only a mountain
A pyramid is just a shape
Doesn't have to hold you back...
Let your dreams take flight...
Did you know that it's true
Everything is possible
There's nothing we can't do"

I highly recommend reading the actual lyrics to "Believe" by Shawn Mendes. They are powerful. I especially connect with the words, "Everything is possible and there's nothing we can't do." If you live your life like this, then the true magic starts happening! You can also go to JoelSalomon.com to listen to "Believe."

October was a tough month for the fund despite my listening to four songs now with "Believe" in the title.

I continued to have lots of doubts about my investing prowess, especially since we had gone another nine months in 2015 and we were barely making money for investors.

When the market has big jumps, a low net strategy like SaLaurMor had a very difficult time out-performing.

October was another month in which the fund *declined* while the market *jumped*.

This was the worst-case scenario for us.

I now had a hard time remembering August and September, when the market dropped 9% and the fund outperformed by almost 12%. The 8% jump in the stock market in October erased all those relative gains.

I believe October was our worst relative month since starting the fund. I restarted my Tapping routine as well in October and tried to do more meditating. This helped me become more centered and less stressed even when we had many down days in a row.

Meditating made me feel more focused and more aware of my surroundings. I remember jogging and noticing the house around my corner. It had white columns like the White House and I had not noticed the columns ever before! I also noticed a tree changing colors—vibrant yellow, orange and red—that there was no way I would have noticed before meditating. I was more mindful!

I also realized I wasn't feeling at all happy doing my "dream job."

As I noted in our investor letter for October (written on November 17th 2015 and online at JoelSalomon.com), the fund had over 400 basis points of negative alpha in October. That is, our individual stock calls were much worse than the overall market's return. This was partly because the insurance index underperformed the overall market, but also because some of our favorite longs were actually down for the month as were a few of our property and casualty insurance favorites.

I realized my happiness was once again conditional—only feeling the joy if I was making money. This amounted to being reliant on external factors for my own happiness.

This is a really important aspect that many, many people don't realize. If you are only going to be happy when an event occurs that "makes" you happy, then you are not really taking responsibility for your life.

If you only feel good or bad, happy or sad, because of physical reality events, then you are not creating your own joy.

What if you decided to be happy independent of external events? What if you decided to wake up every morning and have the attitude that you create your own happiness?

It doesn't matter if it is raining or snowing or sunny or cloudy. The same goes for if you just cut yourself shaving or got a flat tire. This is one of my definitions of being mindful. When you *know* that you create your happiness and you are present in that state, it is really powerful.

What if when something "bad" happened you had the attitude of saying, "Everything happens for a reason" and "From bad things come great things." If you live your life in gratitude and appreciation, then you can be happy—independent of physical events.

If you continue to observe actual events or physical reality rather than anticipate the abundance on its way to you, then you are essentially blocking the abundance—whether it be in money and material things or love and happiness—from coming in. And you are having doubts that you are worthy of abundance and prosperity.

I realize now that the months when the fund was doing poorly, or worse, when the fund was down and the market was up (like October

2015), I was feeling very unhappy. As Rhonda Byrne says so clearly in *The Secret*, when you are feeling depressed or down, you get more events and circumstances in your life to be depressed or down about. That is why it is so important to get your feelings back to gratitude, appreciation, and love.

As Dr. John Hagelin also stated in *The Secret*, "Happier thoughts lead to essentially a happier biochemistry. A happier, healthy body. Negative thoughts and stress have been shown to seriously degrade the body and the functioning of the brain, because it's thoughts and emotions that are continuously reassembling, reorganizing, re-creating our body."

> *"Start thinking happy thoughts and start being happy. Happiness is a feeling state of being. You have your finger on the '***feeling happy***' button. Press it now and keep your finger pressed down on it firmly, no matter what is happening around you"*
>
> — THE SECRET, RHONDA BYRNE

November was a great rebound month for SaLaurMor. The fund generated over 160 basis points of alpha (positive stock selection) and was up for the month while the overall market was essentially flat.

Most importantly, we were in striking distance of having a positive result for the year with another solid month like November. A lot seemed to go right after I was focused on being happy.

Our top ideas rebounded dramatically from October's weak relative and absolute performance. Many of our longs that were sensitive to higher interest rates, jumped. Despite the limited impact on the economic fair value of small moves in the 10-year Treasury note to life insurers and banks, these sectors continued to be highly correlated (they went up when the yield went up) to these small moves. And "because" the 10-year Treasury note jumped more than fifteen basis points in two months, it was no surprise the stocks of life insurers were up 2.9% in November. This was the best-performing insurance sub-sector.

The SaLaurMor portfolio benefitted from this strong outperformance because of our long position in life insurers during the month.

Chapter 15

● ● ●

Making Everyone In This Room Financially Free

Wouldn't it be great to be able to help others?

To help hundreds or thousands of people (or more) become financially free?

To educate them on investments and on the insurance and investment industries?

To help them manifest their dreams and desires?

This is being of service to others.

This is indeed a dream of mine!

With another year coming to a close and the business still not profitable (i.e., we are not able to pay employees market salaries while also funding all the infrastructure costs of a hedge fund from legal to auditing to fund administration), I decided to take a course that sounded like just what I needed to get SaLaurMor to the next level in 2016.

All I had to do was get down to Orlando (frequent flyer miles helped there), and then the course was free except for only a $99 per night fee for the resort.

The description for the weekend was very enticing as well: "Learn how to re-ignite your finances, business, career and relationships. The weekend delivers change that lasts. We provide the real-life tools customized for your personal roadmap to getting results—so that you can live the life you choose." Furthermore, they talked about some of the other things I would learn, including:

* Creating powerful rituals
* Business and branding strategies
* Creating your success formula
* 10x vs. 2x thinking and planning
* Creating an unstoppable team
* Business systemization processes
* Creating action steps

I decided to sign up for the session starting on December 18th and running through December 20th. I was positive it was going to get me ready for a 2016 that would be unparalleled.

I even mentioned the course to a friend of mine, Carl, who lived in Tampa, Florida.

He and I had worked at New York Life Insurance Company together more than twenty-five years ago, but we had kept in touch over the years.

Carl is an extremely caring and thoughtful man. I remember him giving me a book when I wasn't the most avid reader back in the late 1990s called *How to Be Twice as Smart* by Scott Witt. The book was an incredible eye-opener for me.

Without much encouragement from my side, Carl decided to join me in Orlando.

So, I went to Orlando with a completely open mind. Carl decided to take a few precious days away from his beloved family to learn and grow both personally and professionally as well.

There were people from all over Florida, but very few from outside the state. It was the last few days before Christmas and for those who hadn't completed their shopping, the last-minute frenzy was on. So, I was surprised to find almost 200 people in class on Friday, December 18th.

Remember: "Happiness equals reality divided by expectations."

Though I had some expectations, I knew that reality would come in higher and I would be happy.

The first night set the stage for the weekend. Robert, a most engaging speaker, was as fantastic as Doug Nelson had been three years earlier. He also had his share of great quotes for us to live by. His energy was contagious and I knew right away I was in the right place and that I'd made a great decision. I was ready to figure out how to find new investors and set myself up for success in 2016.

Some of his quotes Friday night included:

* "Time is one of your most precious commodities."
* "Everything on this planet/universe is energy."
* "Be the change you want to see in the world."
* "Everything is happening for a reason."
* "Wake up and say (scream) **I love my life!**'"
* "How can I be of service?"
* "If you are not enjoying what you are doing, do something else."
* "The only time you are growing is the un-comfort zone."
* "The greatest gift to give this planet is to be authentic."
* "You model what your parents did."
* "It's not that we dream too high and miss, but we dream too low and hit!"
* "Be clear about what you want."
* "Doubt the doubts!"

Day two and three were also very powerful, providing team-building exercises. The one that really led to my *aha* moment was the one that Robert called "Obstacles are Illusions."

We were each given a wooden board about two and a half inches thick, eight inches long and five inches wide. Imagine everyone's horror as we had to fill out "permission slips." We were told we were going to break the board with our bare hand!

Robert spent at least forty-five minutes explaining how the holder was to hold the board with his hands covered with protective gloves and the "breaker" was to shift his weight forward but only use his palm outstretched. We practiced setting up and shifting our weight and ending up beyond where the holder was holding the piece of wood. Wow, this was really scary. Is it possible to break your wrist? Remember, "Hesitation = pain"?!

We had to literally break it in half with our hand.

On one side, we wrote our biggest obstacle and on the other side we wrote our goal.

I wrote down my biggest obstacle was raising enough money for SaLaurMor Capital to be wildly profitable.

On the other side, I wrote my goal: "Making everyone in this room financially free."

Wow!

Writing that and saying that made me feel so good. I was being of service to others.

What did Robert say success was? "Success is not a thing; it is more a feeling. You feel complete and you feel successful in your relationship or business."

I also realized that my objective and my goal were non sequiturs. The objective of raising enough money for SaLaurMor Capital had nothing to do with "making everyone in the room financially free."

At this course and a few others I have been to over the years, I have found that when the speaker starts talking about stocks and stock options, especially, they explain it in such a way as to make it seem that you can make *a lot* of money in options, but the risk is very limited or nothing at all. I've heard statements such as these:

"Options have unlimited upside."
"You can trade them anywhere."
"You have very little up-front or start-up costs."
"It requires very little time."
"Options are where the rich make their money."

While many of these statements are true, it is also true that options do have significant risks and if you buy an option you can lose your whole investment. And if you sell an option you can lose a lot more than your whole premium. Also, I'm not sure how many of the rich have used stock options alone to make their money.

So the other thing that happened at that course I took in December of 2015 was that other attendees started to ask me questions about stocks and stock options, after our guest speaker had finished his introductory tutorial on the same subject.

I realized that giving recommendations to invest in securities without knowing key information about the attendees—including their risk tolerance, net worth, earnings, cash flow, and investment knowledge—was inappropriate. And I felt this part of the presentation was not authentic and potentially misleading.

Many attendees asked me if stock options were essentially riskless. Please see JoelSalomon.com in the Investing section under Programs for a discussion on stock options for my obvious answer. Some felt they could make multiples of their investment—using leverage. That is certainly true; however, no one discussed the risk of losing their whole investment, which is also possible.

• • •

It dawned on me from all these discussions that education was essential, and I could do a really good job of helping others and being of service to them based on my long history in the insurance and investment industry.

Knowing the limited amount of information most individuals had on investments and the lack of information many have about their own situation, the possibility to help others seemed to be quite large to me. I felt an obligation to help the people in the course and realized there must be many other courses like these which could be hugely beneficial and educational to potential investors, helping them to achieve financial freedom.

I came home from the course knowing my mission in life was *not* investing institutional and high-net worth individuals' money.

I could have continued on investing this money, but it didn't *feel* right. I could have been a super successful hedge fund manager. But what did I do next?

I didn't sleep the night I came home from the course, because that wooden board—actually one half of the board—stared back at me all night: "Make everyone in this room financially free."

I went into my office that Monday morning and informed my investors I was planning on shutting down my hedge fund. This was a major decision that may be hard for you as a reader to understand. A dream that I thought was "right" for twenty years was really not my true purpose in life. I know that may sound a bit cliché, but it's true.

This huge decision to shut down my company came quickly. It was my "higher self" showing me "truth." I knew that trusting this decision was the right thing to do. Remember this was the company I longed to start for years. It was the company I had so much difficulty finding investors for in 2012 and 2013. Recall also, I had two employees I was paying salaries and benefits. Two people who relied on my good judgment. I had two daughters that relied on my cash flow generation for their child support. And of course, I had all the service providers who had supported me unconditionally (though some may say they were more than fairly compensated for their efforts) for almost four years. Was I throwing this all away based on a "whim"?

No!

I began with a simple question:

Is investing my true purpose on earth?

Am I supposed to be helping ultra-high net worth individuals and companies become super-wealthy, or am I supposed to be of service to those in need?

Am I supposed to help those who can really gain by my knowledge and experience?

Shouldn't I help those who can gain not only from my financial acumen, but also from my knowledge that everything depends on your thoughts and if you can "act as if," you can indeed achieve what you ask for?

When I informed my investors that I was going to return their money because I wanted to align my mission with my career, I did not receive significant pushback. This indicated to me that I was on the right track!

In fact, I was quite surprised to not get *any* response to the email I sent to investors in January of 2016 informing them of the closing of the fund. I literally had to leave voicemail messages for our investors before I received a response. Yes, it felt like I was on the right track, but it also made me think how unimportant the fund's returns and performance was to the overall companies and individuals that had invested. I felt like they simply didn't care. I remembered back to the months when we had had terrible performance (according to me at least) down 2% or so and we did not get any response to our investor letters. Clearly, our investors were concerned with more pressing and important matters.

"Our Deepest Fear" by Marianne Williamson

"Our deepest fear is not that we are inadequate. *Our deepest fear is that we are powerful beyond measure.* It is our light, not our darkness that most frightens us. We ask ourselves, "Who am I to be brilliant, gorgeous, talented, fabulous?" Actually, who are you *not* to be? You are a child of God. You're playing small does not serve the world. There is nothing enlightened about shrinking so that other people won't feel insecure around you. We are all meant to shine, as children do. We were born to make manifest the glory of God that is within us. It's not just in some of us; it's in everyone. And as we let our own light shine, we unconsciously give other people permission to do the same. As we are liberated from our own fear, our presence automatically liberates others."

Chapter 16

● ● ●

Prosperity Coaching

*"If something is coming to an end, and you've tried
and given your all and now it's just time, then allow
it to end with grace and gratitude and an open
mind for a new day. No anger. No bitterness. No
need for justification or reward or validation. Just
reverence for this time, for the whispers of renewal."*

—BRENDON BURCHARD

As we began the process of selling securities to close down the fund, I knew this was the right decision. I figured out that being of service to others and helping people become financially free was inconsistent with my managing a hedge fund. I started a Meetup group that focused on helping others achieve their goals and dreams by changing their mindset around money, while also getting them to save ("pay yourself first"), and then ultimately to invest.

So, what were my lessons learned while I had my "dream job"? They are numerous:

1. **Enjoy yourself and have fun.** I realized there were many days I didn't enjoy the daily requirements of raising capital or networking. I came to realize that the more you are present—in the moment, being mindful and enjoying what you are doing (from the mundane to the boring)—the more abundance will flow to you.

2. **Doubt the doubts.** Throughout the process of raising capital, analyzing companies and producing investment returns for investors, I had doubts about my capabilities. Why should the doubts be correct? Doubt them!

3. **"Act as if."** As Author Sandy Forster calls it, "Be, Do, then Have." When you act as if you have already achieved your goals and dreams, you feel abundant, happy and successful. That feeling will translate into doing whatever it takes—and then of course, you will have the abundance or goal you'd been striving for. We did this both times we were about to raise capital, and it worked wonders.

4. **You are responsible for your life and all aspects of life.** I truly believe everything happens for a reason. I was able to realize my dream and my dream job, which led me to a new dream, the one I'm realizing now.

5. **The more you give, the more you get.** But most importantly, doing things for others feels good and is the right thing to do.

6. **You have a right to be rich!** Wallace Wattles says, in *The Science of Getting Rich*, "Whatever may be said in praise of poverty, the fact remains that it is not possible to live a really complete or successful life unless one is rich. No man can rise to his greatest possible height in talent or soul development

unless he has plenty of money; for *to unfold the soul and develop talent* he must have many things to use, and he cannot have these things unless he has money to buy them with."

7. And yes, as Mike Dooley says, **thoughts become things!**

Colin Powell, the former four-star General in the U.S. Army and Secretary of State from 2001 through 2005, said this about money: "Look for something you love to do and you do well. Go for it. It will give you satisfaction in life. It could mean money, but it may not. It could mean a lot of titles, but it may not. But it will give you satisfaction."

In *Your Erroneous Zones*, Wayne Dyer stated: "You are behaving as a fool if you look outside of you for an explanation of how you should feel or what you should do. Taking credit, as well as responsibility for yourself, is the first step in eliminating this erroneous zone. Be your own hero."

Today I am an Infinite Possibilities (IP) Trainer and Prosperity Coach. I work with people who are interested in becoming financially free while taking full responsibility for their future and learning how to create major life changes. The IP training was created by Mike Dooley with the belief that everyone is special, every life is meaningful, and we're all here to learn that dreams really do come true.

In 2016, I began working with individuals I met in my Meetup group or from personal recommendations. Initially, I worked with folks who wanted to become better educated about individual stock investing. They wanted to know what the definitions of market capitalization, price-to-earnings ratio, price-to-book value ratio, dividend payout ratio and other similar terms were. They also wanted to know how these ratios were used by investors. These initial clients were quite fearful about the stock market and I worked with them on their money mindset as well.

One of my clients had not invested in the stock market. So, we were really starting from the very basics. He eventually transitioned to a paper trading portfolio in which he used fake money to see how his trading and investing would have done if he had invested real money. I also started a program with him to improve his cash flow by paying down high-interest debt obligations (mostly student loans and credit cards). Finally, he began to "pay himself first" (see Chapter 2 for how I did it).

Another early client was trading currencies using a proprietary program he had developed and back-tested. The results of his back-testing were impressive and the first few months of using his system were quite profitable, but when he came to me, he had lost a lot of money and was living in fear of losing it all. We worked closely together on his fear and doubt, shifting them to belief and self-confidence. He had recently been making decisions purely on emotion; effectively doing the opposite of what his proprietary program would have been recommending, all because of his fear.

Working with these initial clients was so rewarding. It really helped me to recognize that this kind of work can be truly helpful to others.

Another client, who I will call Jay, had a scarcity mindset (also known as "poverty consciousness") when in fact he was generating significant monthly cash flow. He had saved and invested, and though mostly retired, his passive income was enough to cover his expenses. He came to me saying "I am running out of money."

In his mind, this was indeed the case. But in reality his cash flow from the prior year was only negative because he had used cash to buy a new car and also fund his art studio. I showed him how, if he backed these one-time expenses out, his actual cash flow last year was more than $50,000 to the positive. This client was not willing to share his actual net worth with me, but I estimated he would be unlikely to outlive his money for the next twenty years, while his life expectancy was about fifteen. Jay is my ideal client: He is open-minded. He had been schooled in the teachings of Esther Hicks, Louise Hay, and many other spiritual writers and speakers, yet his mindset was not set for success, but it could be changed easily.

I also work with clients on mindfulness and intuition. As I have become more mindful about money, I've found what an important part emotions play in making money. Fear and doubt definitely hinder lucrative opportunities while happiness, gratitude and appreciation attract them. If a client is quite fearful about investing in stocks and mutual funds, and that area is not a passion, then we don't start there. Overcoming limiting beliefs around investing is the first step to financial freedom in my humble opinion.

From my experience, intuition is also very important to achieving your dreams and desires. As I already noted, when I followed my intuition, my gut, my "sixth sense"—I either made more money or lost less.

So, it *is* important to develop your intuition or gut feeling as much as possible.

How do you do that?

First, use it as often as possible. I've tried to use these hunches whenever I feel them, even with small amounts of money. It can also apply to non-monetary decisions.

If you have to make a decision whether to stay on a highway or get off at the nearest exit, try not to use Google Maps! Which way is your intuition telling you to go? Go with it!

Another way to develop your intuition is through meditation. I have discussed this in Chapter 9 and noted you can use meditation or a guided meditation to simply quiet your mind.

Using positive affirmations while you meditate is also quite powerful. Say out loud or to yourself, "I am a money magnet" or "lucrative opportunities come my way." See the rest of T. Harv Eker's declarations on my website at JoelSalomon.com. Also, feel free to email me for some of the powerful money affirmations I do daily.

I also started giving everyone I met a one-hour free prosperity coaching session.

This allowed me to help a large number of people, to some extent, while giving the many people in my Meetup group access to me without having to pay.

I set out a course for all these entrepreneurial people to "pay themselves first" and work on getting their expenses in line with their income.

I also helped them set up an emergency expense account covering at least three to six months' worth of their ordinary expenses.

I've developed three stand-alone modules for those I work with, though some have gone through all three modules and find them intertwined (for example, when they are taught about manifesting they can use that knowledge to invest in stocks). Some clients were solely interested in learning the basics of stock and stock options investing. Others were interested in bonds, stop losses and mutual funds. The first module teaches you all you ever wanted to know about all these subjects but were afraid to ask.

The second module teaches you all you ever wanted to know about manifesting. I've previously discussed how "thoughts becomes things" and getting more of what you want—and quicker in Chapter 2. There I described some amazing experiences at Citi. In this module, you are taught some important money affirmations and declarations along with how to tell whether you are poverty-conscious or prosperity-conscious. You are given some money self-talks as well as ways to overcome your money blocks and how to visualize in the appropriate way.

The third module covers how to become financially free, and defines your financial freedom number plus your cash flow and net worth. You are taught new habits about savings and spending. For many people, just getting out of debt is a huge step. But we also teach the specifics around "paying yourself first" and the difference between "credit and debt."

I am living the life of my dreams and working with others to help them achieve the same. I feel so happy to be helping others, knowing it is my true purpose here on earth.

Follow your bliss!

Are you interested in developing these thoughts more deeply?

Are you interested in moving toward financial freedom?

Do you want to learn more about how to overcome adversity to have financial freedom?

Do you want to start "Acting as if?"

Please go online to JoelSalomon.com to start yourself on your way to financial freedom. I believe in you!

Thanks for reading! If you loved the book (or even liked it) and have a moment to spare, I would really appreciate a short review as this helps new readers find my books.

Appendix 1

• • •

My Top Five Cities in the United States

My top has to be New York City. Though I no longer live there, the experience of having worked there almost every day of my career (except in 1999 and 2000) allowed me to have experienced what most people in the world only dream about.

As I have told many of the people I meet and coach who live and work there, "You are living the dream of more than 99% of the world who would love to be in your shoes and walk the streets of one of the most unique, awe-inspiring cities in the world." It is dripping with culture from Broadway shows to museums, and of course it may be one of the most diverse cities in the world.

I have had interactions with people from Nepal, Bangladesh, India, Singapore, Egypt, Brazil, Chile, Australia, and New Zealand, all in one day! New York City may have the most five-star Michelin restaurants in the world, with over seventy-five in 2017.

For me, the diversity of restaurants is just so amazing. When a date recommended an Ethiopian restaurant in the late 1990s, I was not at all surprised that there was one on the Upper East Side of Manhattan (now there are more than ten!).

In fact, if you want to eat authentic, world-class Japanese (sushi is one of my top ten meals) one night and Greek the next—then Italian, Chinese, German, Mexican, French, Indian, Brazilian, Korean, Spanish, Middle Eastern, and of course, American BBQ—you could! I know some people who have gone a whole month in New York City, enjoying dishes from a different cuisine every day!

Now, since this is a book about a former hedge fund manager, another reason that NYC is my favorite is because it is home to such a huge concentration of both financial and intellectual capital.

One of my favorite aspects of investing has been meeting with all the companies that we were investing in. Many of the Chief Executive Officers (CEOs) and Chief Financial Officers (CFOs) of these companies are among the smartest people I've met throughout my life. Some of my favorites are ones who manage large asset managers and private equity firms. A few insurance company CEOs would also top the list, such as Evan Greenberg of The Chubb Corporation.

The largest money manager in the world, BlackRock, has its headquarters at Park Avenue and 52nd Street. BNY Mellon Investment Management and J.P. Morgan Asset Management are also in the top ten globally in terms of assets under management. Blackstone, the largest private equity money manager, is not far away, also on Park Avenue. Other large money managers include Goldman Sachs Asset Management and AB, formerly Alliance Bernstein, and a subsidiary of AXA Investment Advisers, which is in turn a subsidiary of AXA, a large French insurer. In total, one could say over $11 trillion is managed from Manhattan!

My other favorite cities besides New York are San Francisco, New Orleans, Nashville, and the "city" of Lahaina on Maui in Hawaii.

San Francisco is so unique because of its Golden Gate Bridge, views of the ocean, and also it being a gateway to the East. I remember going to the Golden Gate Park the first time in 1998. The park definitely rivals Central Park as my favorite common area in the United States. You can visit the Japanese Tea Garden which was originally constructed in 1893. It has a 1.5-ton Buddha, a moon bridge, and the first fortune cookies were created and served in the Teahouse in 1914.

There are bridle paths and over seven thousand kinds of plants, along with unique trees like the Redwood. You can also see a unique view of Mount Tamalpais and the Golden Gate Bridge from Strawberry Hill.

While San Francisco's financial sector is smaller than New York's, it is home to Wells Fargo, one of the largest banks in the U.S., as well as a large venture capital industry which has helped finance the growth of Silicon Valley. And the technology boom continues in Silicon Valley while the internet start-ups have followed Google, which is based in Santa Clara near San Jose, not far from San Francisco.

My first visit to San Francisco was bittersweet. I was going with a girlfriend whom I had broken up with earlier in the year (1998). She was hoping to convince me that we should get back together and at least date again. I ultimately agreed to make the trip, figuring it would be fun to go with someone rather than go alone. Besides, I had frequent flyer miles running out that year and decided to use them to tour San Francisco, since I had only seen the inside of a San Francisco conference room when I worked at Moody's.

I've learned a lot about myself since then—my strengths, and indeed, the fact I should grab any improvement opportunities which arise.

But back in the day, my own insecurity was in big need of an improvement opportunity. So, when Sue started speaking with another couple that first morning at a local breakfast joint, I became quite upset.

Wasn't I interesting enough to talk to?

Why would you start talking to strangers, *ever*?

My view has changed now, and in fact, you probably will find me talking more to strangers on trips than people I already know.

I enjoy learning their backgrounds, their stories, and why they live there. I am also confident enough to know that I, like everyone else, am interesting to converse with on most topics.

The trip was pretty much downhill from there (no pun intended since the café was not on Lombard Street!), though we did manage to get to Napa Valley and enjoy some awesome-tasting Mondavi and Beringer wines.

New Orleans is much, much smaller than New York and San Francisco, but it has to be on my list of top five U.S. cities to visit.

The music on Bourbon Street is first-rate, especially for those who love their blues and jazz.

The Big Easy has great restaurants, serving its distinctive local cuisine, and bars with a lively music scene almost every night. For a seafood lover, the Étouffée makes the trip worthwhile. Though I have not been there for Mardi Gras, which is usually during earnings season in mid-February, the town is alive year-round. The history of "N'Orlins" (as pronounced by the locals) reflects its origins with a mix of French, African, and American influences.

At times, one can feel that they're in a different country because of the strong French influence.

I've been to N.O. a few times but the first time was for a Society of Actuaries meeting in 2002. I went with my fiancée at the time. We enjoyed a day before and after the meeting exploring the city. We appreciated the great music and even some unusual museums including the N.O. Historic Voodoo Museum, the Pharmacy Museum, along with the more traditional N.O. Museum of Art.

It was also interesting to see the Cabildo, the seat of the Spanish colonial government. The original building was destroyed in 1788 by a fire, but the Baroque architecture remains unique on Chartres Street.

For those readers who are foodies and don't care about calorie counts, the beignets at Café Du Monde are a must. These fried fritters made of dough and covered with powdered sugar are not the healthiest, but certainly a unique experience. And one I make sure to have each trip to the Big Easy.

Another music city that I have to include on the list is Nashville, Tennessee. The influence of the Grand Ole Opry House which made Nashville for many, many years the music capital of the U.S. (mostly because it had the strongest radio signal in the South until the early 1990s) is profound.

Elvis' influence is also huge, having recorded his music at the RCA Victor Studio B for a full twenty years between 1957 and 1977.

Nashville has its own Broadway, though there aren't any major musicals there. It does, however, boast great bars including the famous Honky Tonk.

One shouldn't miss the Country Music Hall of Fame and Museum or Studio B. The original Grand Ole Opry—the Ryman Auditorium, deserves a look as well. Finally, the Bluebird Café provides a unique view of up-and-coming singers/songwriters.

My last city in the top five is really not a town at all. I have to include one of the most beautiful islands in the world: Maui. The lovely turquoise water and the sunsets are reason enough to visit. But I would add the Haleakala volcano, the aquarium with the shark tank, and visiting the more than thirty miles of beaches as well.

Maui is a place I am really looking forward to visiting again with Lauren and Morgan, in the near future. I remember taking a helicopter ride over the beautiful island, and seeing amazing cliffs and waterfalls. I also recall the required late-night (or early-morning for some) drive to the Haleakala Volcano so you could get there by sunrise. That view was unforgettable. Snorkeling was also amazing there because of all the amazing colors of fish and sea turtles. I know

Lauren and Morgan would enjoy them, given their passion for fish and animals.

So, my top five cities in the U.S. are New York City, San Francisco, New Orleans, Nashville, and Maui. Clearly, different readers will have different preferences based on their own personal likes and dislikes, desires and distastes. Be mindful and think about what would be your top five. Maybe they are completely different than mine, or similar. Go there! Explore!

Appendix 2

● ● ●

My Top Five Cities in Europe

In no particular order, though Rome and Paris are probably neck-and-neck, the following are my top five cities in Europe.

Rome is an open-air museum. The Roman Forum is almost 3000 years old. It is where Julius Caesar spoke around fifty years before Christ. He also built the Basilica Julia along with the Curia Julia, refocusing both the judicial offices and the Senate. Some of the 2000 year-old temples are very well preserved. The Coliseum is almost 2000 years old and a massive stone amphitheater that hosted gladiator fights. I remember being completely awestruck upon seeing a building so much older than anything in the U.S. It was unreal to simply walk down the street and encounter stones or artifacts over one thousand years old.

Rome also has the Vatican, a city unto itself. I remember looking up at the ceiling of the Sistine Chapel, built between 1473 and 1481, and being overcome with joy. Its ceiling has nine panels depicting scenes from the Book of Genesis.

Rome has a really bad reputation in some circles. Some people consider it dirty. Others consider it unsafe. Some complain of pickpockets and scams to take tourists' money. I'm sure one can find some story about each major city in the world including my favorite U.S. city, New York. I found Rome to be neither dirty nor risky when I first went there in 1999. And it felt safe as well on my most recent visit in 2015.

Getting around without being fluent in Italian might have been my biggest stumbling block. But this also allowed me to try out my limited language capabilities with the locals. So, I remember walking from my hotel to the Spanish Steps, the famous shopping area in Rome, and getting lost. However, some nice local man was able to give me directions in his broken English and helped me get there despite the time lost. This experience not only showed me the kindness inherent in others—but that yet again—from bad things come good things.

Paris is another of my favorite destinations. How could it not be, with the best food and wine in Europe?

Paris boasts more than 70 five-star Michelin restaurants. It may be the only city in the world besides New York City to hold that distinction.

The Eiffel Tower, built in 1887 by Gustave Eiffel, is the tallest building in Paris at 324 meters or about 1062 feet. I had a hard time not taking a picture of it wherever I was in the city.

In fact, I may have taken more than 500 pictures of the Tower at various times of the day—morning, noon, and night—from hundreds of vantage points throughout the city including The Cathedral of Notre Dame!

My most interesting memory of Notre Dame is the gargoyles at the top of the Cathedral. I climbed 387 steps to get a really close-up view of them! Some are laughing, while others are spitting, grimacing, or looking bored. Why were they made?

What purpose do they serve?

Some questions for the ages!

The Cathedral took over 300 years to build and has been remembered as, among other things, the place where Joan of Arc was posthumously blessed by Pope Pius in 1909.

Paris also has amazing museums such as the Louvre. This is home to Leonardo da Vinci's 500-year-old painting of the Mona Lisa. For someone who is not an art aficionado, spending over five hours in the Louvre is saying something!

The famous sculpture of *The Thinker* can be found at the Rodin Museum. The Picasso Museum also calls Paris home.

And of course, Paris is celebrated for one of the most famous shopping streets in all of Europe—the Champs Elysees.

When I first visited Paris in 1995 with Rob and Ken, it was just so special.

I remember, though, also having to deal with a big loss. My father's mother was sick and in the hospital when I left on my trip. But to me at least, she didn't seem like she was on her deathbed.

Maybe it was just her putting on her normal smiley face and positive air, but while I was gone, her health took a quick turn for the worse. I received a call from my Dad on the second day of our time in Paris to tell me she had died. He said it was up to me whether to return home for the funeral or continue on my journey.

My paternal grandmother was the grandparent I was closest to. She lived in East Rockaway, New York just twenty-five minutes from my parents and about forty-five minutes from where I was living at the time, Commack. So, I would see her often—at least twice a month in the early 1990s after her husband had passed away.

This was a really tough decision and I remember praying on it. I wasn't, and am not now, a religious individual. Temple was a part of my life growing up, but I was quite skeptical about the whole existence of God. I liked how, as Jews, it was okay to say we are searching for an answer instead of being required to just unconditionally believe.

I stayed up that night praying for an answer for what to do. I think I was really hoping for my recently deceased Grandmother Millie to make a ghostly appearance in downtown Paris and say it was OK to stay.

Whether she did or not I don't honestly remember. What I do know is that when I woke up from the limited sleep I did get that night, I decided that she would have wanted me to continue on with my first European vacation. So, I informed my Dad, and without any guilt, continued on my vacation.

I do believe now that it was the right decision. It is best to live your life and be mindful.

My Grandma Millie was a great cook (especially Hungarian Goulash, tongue, and my favorite, cheesecake). She was a loving mother and grandmother, and a very giving individual. In 1994 and 1995, we spent many Sunday evenings eating her favorite deli sandwich at Katz's deli in Woodmere. She taught me so many life lessons. And almost twenty years after her death, I think about her almost every day.

I will always love Paris, but Bruges is just so unique.

Bruges has been dubbed the Venice of the North. It is about a one-hour train ride from Brussels, Belgium. I had to be in Brussels for a business trip in July 1999 and was able to visit Bruges for a day trip on a Saturday. Wow! What a day it was!

Bruges has a great Market or square, a romantic canal like Venice where you can rent boats, and it has been around for almost 900 years. But what is so interesting about Bruges is that it has most of its medieval architecture intact. This makes it one of the most preserved medieval towns in Europe. In Bruges, you will find the sculpture of *Madonna and Child* by Michelangelo, which is believed to be the only sculpture that left Italy during his lifetime.

Prague, the capital of the Czech Republic, is another one of my favorite cities. I visited Prague with a group of New York and Swiss friends and colleagues in 1999.

We had a great long weekend. We visited the Prague castle, which is the largest ancient castle in the world, occupying an area of almost 70,000 square meters or about 750,000 square feet. It is a must-see. The history of the castle began in 870 when its first walled building was built. Two basilicas were founded in the 900s, making parts of the Castle over 1000 years old. The Charles Bridge is over 600 years old and it is decorated by a continuous alley of thirty statues and statuaries in old Baroque style. The original statues were made over 300 years ago.

My friends and colleagues kept on pulling me away as I didn't want to leave without getting a picture of each statue. Prague also has a unique Jewish quarter with an interesting cemetery and great beer, including the original Budweiser brand.

Finally, I would be remiss if I didn't mention my second home, Zurich.

I lived in Zurich for almost a year and a half.

When I visited Zurich in January 1999, a colleague of mine at Swiss Re, happened to be "working out" at the Luxor Sports Club (affiliated with New York Sports Club at the time) and introduced himself to me as a fellow New Yorker.

Tom and I became fast friends and one weekend he offered to take me on a tour of Zurich. We started with the Grossmunster. I don't remember much of the art gallery in that museum because we spent most of the time getting into a deep conversation over past girl-friends and actuarial experiences. The Grossmunster's Twin Towers, built almost 900 years ago, did provide an amazing panoramic view of the city, though.

We also visited the Fraumunster, another beautiful church, which was built over 1000 years ago. Impressive Chagall windows, that were worked on throughout the 1960s and have been on view since 1970, are a key attraction.

While dripping with culture, Zurich is also a lot of fun. Swim in the lake in the summer. Take a boat ride on Lake Zurich. Enjoy amazing hiking trails (I was able to run up most of Uetliberg Mountain some lunch hours). Ski within forty-five minutes of the city center!

These five cities belong on every bucket list and are my top five European cities.

But a trip to Istanbul, Turkey was one of my most unique experiences.

I expected to really experience the "Middle East," but what I felt was the intertwining of multiple worlds, as befits a city that straddles two continents, and served as the capital of both the (Eastern) Roman and Ottoman Empires. It felt like the Old World and New World occupied separate parts of the city and you could easily move from one to the other.

I vividly remember getting into a taxicab at the airport and asking for an estimate of how much it would cost to get to our hotel. The cab driver gave us an estimate of 44 million Turkish Lira! This worked out to just over twenty U.S. dollars given the weak Lira at that time.

We stayed at the wonderful Swissotel. Thanks to a favorable currency exchange rate, coupled with the experience of looking out the window and seeing the Bosphorus, the $350-a-night room was well worth the expense.

I also remember going to the Blue Mosque for the first time and seeing hundreds, perhaps thousands, of men kneel on the red carpet at the call to prayer. The Mosque was built over 500 years ago and has over 200 stained glass windows and lots of chandeliers. There is marble everywhere you can look and the dome itself is almost 150 feet high.

Other highlights of our trip were the boat ride on the Bosphorus, and eating sensational seafood and delicious kebabs from street vendors during the day.

We also spent hours walking through the Spice Bazaar. The haggling that went on in the Bazaar was some of the most intense I had experienced in my life. And I've now seen picky portfolio managers trying to get a stock an eighth of a point or 12.5 cents cheaper!

The guides made it clear that no price was set. We were expected to bargain. But being a tough negotiator wasn't a known strength of mine. Thanks to my colleague, who had a background in law, the deals we negotiated were legendary. He bought a beautiful carpet that I believe was more than 60% off of the original ask.

Appendix 3

●　●　●

Weight Loss

knew shedding the extra weight I was carrying around would be easy if I simply got back into my routine of eating properly and exercising.

The weight-loss contest with the analyst ran through June 21st, just in time for the first day of summer. That meant I had about two months to lose the fifteen pounds; though I would have to lose more if my opponent lost more.

In Rhonda Byrne's best-selling book *The Secret*, the author discusses how to use the Law of Attraction to lose weight.

First, you *ask*. You ask yourself what is your ideal weight. You get a strong mental picture of yourself at your perfect weight. Or you get pictures of the body you would like to have and you look at it often.

Then you *believe*. You must envision yourself at the perfect weight. You write out your perfect weight and place it over your scale. You look through catalogues of clothes that you will wear at your perfect weight. You praise people who have your idea of the perfect bodies. You admire them.

Then you *receive*. You must feel good about yourself. Feel good now. Byrne also mentions Wallace Wattles, the author of *The Science of Getting Rich*. In Wattles' book, he recommends "When you eat, make sure you are entirely focused on the experience of chewing the food. Keep your mind present and experience the sensation of eating food, and do not allow your mind to drift to other things."

Byrne tells us she is convinced that when we are present and mindful, "Entirely focused on the pleasurable experience of eating, the food is assimilated into our bodies perfectly, and the result in our bodies *must* be perfection."

I definitely *knew* this was going to be easy. I *knew* I could attain my college weight. I had not even started and I already felt good about it.

I did not do the Wattles technique, though I did use Rhonda's. I have met people who do, and they all seem to be quite thin. My cousin, Marc Trager, is the slowest eater I know besides my grandfather, Milton Salomon. Marc tips the scales at just 20 pounds more than me despite being more than 6 inches taller.

What did I do to lose the weight?

The most important things were:

1. Exercise. I began to do sit-ups and push-ups almost every morning. I began with twenty sit-ups, twenty leg lifts and twenty push-ups. I kept on adding more and eventually by

the end of the two months, I was doing sixty sit-ups, sixty leg lifts and sixty push-ups. I also began jogging again every other weekend. I started jogging two days every other weekend for fifteen minutes. Then I managed three days a week for thirty minutes or about three miles.

2. Eating healthy. I changed my breakfast meal from a bowl of sugar-laden cereal to orange juice, oatmeal and a banana. I stopped eating sandwiches for lunch. Instead, I opted for salads and fresh fruit. I effectively reduced my carbohydrates by not eating bread at lunch and limiting my pasta in the evenings as well.

3. Choosing beverages wisely. At least once a day I was downing a Dr. Pepper with the dreaded high-fructose corn syrup. At first, I trimmed that daily habit down to one five days a week. Ultimately I cut it out completely and just had three 1-liter bottles of water daily. I also stopped drinking alcohol four to five days a week. I limited myself to one glass of wine two nights a week.

And to be completely open with you, I did fast the last night of the weight loss challenge to make sure I did indeed take those fifteen pounds off.

Long story short, I lost seventeen pounds by June 21st and have kept most of that weight off.

About the Author

Joel Salomon is a prosperity coach who helps others overcome obstacles standing in the way of their financial freedom. In 2012, he achieved a decades-long dream with the launch of his own hedge fund, SaLaurMor Capital (named after his two daughters, Lauren and Morgan).

Salomon's financial experience includes managing long/short equity and credit portfolios for Citi, with an emphasis on asset managers, insurers, and specialty financial companies. Salomon generated positive returns every year during his time at Citi, including 2008, when the market suffered 40 percent losses.

Salomon has been a Chartered Financial Analyst since 1995. In 1992, he was named a Fellow of the Society of Actuaries.

When not helping others achieve their financial dreams, Salomon enjoys table tennis, bowling, and skiing. He is also an avid traveler and has visited over forty countries and five continents.

Made in the USA
Middletown, DE
16 October 2018